DAVID IREDALE AND JOHN BARRETT

D1311142

Discovering
Your Family Tree

A pocket guide to tracing your ancestors
and compiling your family history

SHIRE PUBLICATIONS LTD

Contents

For Emma Barrett

Copyright © 1985 by David Iredale and John Barrett. 'Discovering Your Family Tree' by David Iredale first published 1970; second edition 1973, reprinted 1975, 1976; third edition 1977, reprinted 1979, 1980, 1981, 1983; this fourth edition, completely revised, updated and rewritten by David Iredale and John Barrett, first published 1985, reprinted 1987. Number 93 in the Discovering series. ISBN 0 85263 767 5.

Set in 9 point Times roman and printed in Great Britain by C. I. Thomas & Sons (Haverfordwest) Ltd, Press Buildings, Merlins Bridge, Haverfordwest.

1. Family history and genealogy

'Tinker, tailor, soldier, sailor, rich man ...' The child's chant might be a list of the occupations to be found in the family history — or just as likely: 'poor man, beggar man, thief'.

It is always pleasant to discover a branch of the pedigree leading back to a royal ancestor (in 1911 the progeny of Edward III was estimated at one hundred thousand). And indeed, if the searcher is selective enough, carefully picking his way among the branches of the family tree — jumping from limb to limb — he may trace a line back to William the Conqueror — or through him to Woden or Adam.

Genealogies may be used to support many different kinds of snobbery: of the Scot glorying in the peasant squalor of his crofting forebears; the feminist claiming a spurious political awareness for a female ancestor burned as a witch; the socialist ashamed at the discovery of his descent, not from a hanged cattle thief but from the legitimate younger son of a peer. But a modern family is not more worthy for being descended from a noble bastard; and many genealogists will be equally proud of a family tree rooted among the labourers, craftsmen and peasants who have tilled Britain's soil, created the nation's wealth and fought the kings' wars down the years.

Many genealogists will be able to trace their ancestry back through a dozen generations, spanning perhaps three centuries, to produce a pedigree containing a thousand names — or more if the descendants of sisters, cousins and aunts are traced. Every name on the family tree was once a living man or woman and, by studying documentary sources, the family historian may construct detailed biographies to revivify an ancestor and his or her world.

Family history is inseparable from local and national history. The economic condition of the nation or the locality will be a factor in the changing fortunes of the family. The labour of men and women, housing conditions, domestic comforts, leisure pursuits, forms of worship, sexual relations, marital alliances, dress, diet and morality are the products of time and place. And so the genealogist, studying the lives of individuals — their thoughts, actions and motivations — achieves a close understanding of the past.

Genealogical research answers (and sometimes raises) questions about one's self. Hair colour, complexion, stature and facial features are the products of genetics. Other attributes — personality, intelligence, gifts of art or music — are transmitted by a more subtle process from one's forebears.

The family historian requires few special qualifications: patience, application, the self-discipline to adhere to the rules and methods of research, and an enthusiasm for the past — to enjoy the process of detection or the thrill of revelation.

Some genealogists concentrate on a one-line pedigree, tracing the male line backwards from child to father through the generations of a single surname. Or a genealogy may investigate the female line, which introduces a new surname at each generation — and is likely to be more reliable than a male pedigree, for in most cases the genealogist has to take on trust that the children of a marriage have been sired by their mother's husband.

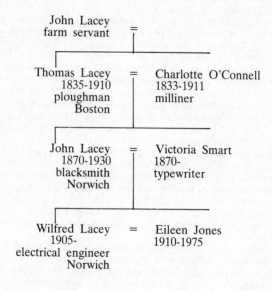

John Lacey
farm servant =

Thomas Lacey = Charlotte O'Connell
1835-1910 1833-1911
ploughman milliner
Boston

John Lacey = Victoria Smart
1870-1930 1870-
blacksmith typewriter
Norwich

Wilfred Lacey = Eileen Jones
1905- 1910-1975
electrical engineer
Norwich

An alternative technique is for the searcher to begin from himself and produce an ever expanding chart of parents, grandparents, great-grandparents, etc.

name of compiler ....

address ....

date ....

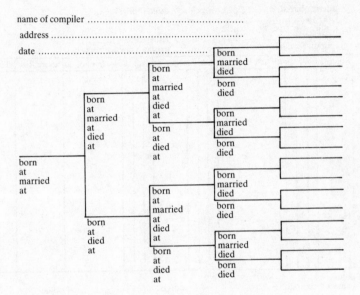

A family group sheet can be compiled for each nuclear family:

sources of information ....
man's name .... wife's maiden name ....
  residence .... residence ....
  birth (baptism) .... birth (baptism) ....
  at .... at ....
  marriage .... other marriages to ....
  at ....
  death (burial) .... death (burial) ....
  at .... at ....
  other marriages to ....
  father's name .... father's name ....
  mother's maiden name .... mother's maiden name ....

children	date born (baptised) at			date married at			date died (buried) at			married to	chart
1											
2											
3											
4											
5											
6											
7											
8											
9											
10											
11											
12											
13											
14											

notes
name of compiler   address   date

This can be illustrated by a simple branch pedigree:

```
                    ┌──────────────────┐
                    │                  │
Alexander Auldpotts = Margaret Milne
'Tinker Caird'
1788 - 1816
farmer
Nairnshire
                                   │
   ┌──────┬──────────┬─────twins──────┬──────────────────┐
Margaret   James      Perdita    Portia     Alexander   = Catherine Gordon
Auldpotts  Auldpotts  Auldpotts  Auldpotts  Auldpotts
1805-      1808-      1810-      1810-      1816-
before 1816 before 1816 before 1816 before 1816  after 1881
                                              pedlar
                                              Moray
                                                 │
              ┌──────────────────────────────────────────
```

But eventually the charts and pedigrees will be combined to produce a family tree.

Nine rules for drawing pedigrees

1. Be consistent in the use of symbols on all charts.
2. Record all members of each generation horizontally in line across the chart (so that the range of occupations, locations, surnames, social classes, lifespans, etc, may be seen at a glance).
3. Record siblings in order of birth.
4. Record dates of birth and death, principal occupation(s) and residence(s) beneath each individual's full name.
5. Draw lines of descent from the marriage symbol.
6. Do not permit pedigree lines to intersect.
7. Record and number successive marriages and genealogically productive liaisons chronologically.
8. Leave space(s) for the addition of information not yet discovered.
9. Record researcher's name and date of compilation.

But a mere pedigree is a lifeless skeleton — an illustration to accompany the written history of the whole family or a series of individual biographies. Historical biography, though requiring no special skill, does demand a large degree of care and organisation. Every step in the research (whether productive or not) should be recorded in a register of sources indicating where and when information was found.

REGISTER OF SOURCES

search number	name and address of source	documents	date of search
1	John Smith, 10 Wills Street, Birmingham, personal visit.	Smith family papers in carton in sideboard 1/1 birth certificate of Adelaide Smith 1852 1/2 photograph of Adelaide Smith c 1870	10 March 1985
2	Moray District Record Office, Tolbooth, Forres, Moray.	Banff burgh archive 2/1 George Shearer tailor in Banff, 1850 (DED BBb A71/850/7)	13 March 1985

For each individual family member whose life is researched in detail a file should be opened. On the file cover a prepared sheet will give brief details of the subject (Mabel Auldpotts, Bexhill, 1888-1984). Inside the file are collected all the sources for an individual's biography: photocopies of documents, copy photographs, typed transcriptions of interviews, newspaper cuttings, and notes from documentary sources or printed books — each marked clearly with its source-list number. The information collected must never be edited — not the expletives used by grandfather in describing his military career, nor the malicious insinuations of a great-aunt's correspondence — for even a mistaken, false, indecorous or obscene statement may add to the searcher's knowledge of an ancestor's character.

When studying in libraries or record offices notes should be written in pencil, on one side only of large (A4 or foolscap) lined paper. A separate page should be used for each new source. Abbreviations and symbols should be employed sparingly. Permitted symbols include: b, birth; ba, baptism (christening); m or =, marriage; l or ≠, extramarital liaison; d, death, di, burial (interment); *c,* circa.

In transcribing documents and other sources spelling, punctuation, capitalisation, italicisation etc must be copied exactly. But the searcher may find a battery-operated cassette-recorder useful for recording interviews as well as for capturing emotional responses during a visit to an ancestor's home, workplace or grave. A typewriter produces more legible fair copies of research notes, but much care is needed when transcriptions of documents are recopied and it is as well also to preserve all original notes.

A card index, alphabetically arranged, of persons, places and subjects mentioned in the source notes can be helpful.

> IRVINE, Reverend James
> Craigness
> employer of Mabel Auldpotts during 1902
> *see* Mabel Auldpotts file
> enclosure number 25
> register of sources number 17

Nor should the researcher be unaware of the potential of the home computer for storing and collating data.

2. Public libraries and other institutions

The search for ancestry begins in the reference, family history and local studies sections of the public library. Books on genealogy and family history should be available on the library shelves or through the inter-library loans service, though the serious genealogist will also wish to purchase a selection of the most helpful guides for his own reference shelf.

Branches of the family may have been researched already and a published family history may be listed in a printed bibliography or library catalogue. But these histories are not always trustworthy, being based on suspect (often unidentified) sources, legends and hearsay; or perhaps snobbery or false rectitude may have resulted in outright fabrication of the pedigree. Every generation of such a pedigree should be researched again line by line.

Nobility and landed gentry

Among the earliest pedigrees were those compiled for the landed class of Tudor and Stuart England. Heralds travelled the shires recording pedigrees and arms; but most of the information was collected from unauthenticated and oral sources. Transcripts of heralds' visitations have been published by local record societies.

Pedigrees of the peerage, baronetage, knightage, companionage and landed gentry appear in the various editions of Debrett (since 1802) and Burke (1826), which provide a summary of the family history, arms, motto and residences, with the names of collateral branches. Biographies of peers and their immediate families appear in *The Complete Peerage* (1910-59).

Heraldry

The family crest engraved on a child's silver christening mug has come a long way from the flamboyantly adorned helmets of medieval warriors in the melée. Crests, escutcheons and mottoes associated with family and clan names are reproduced commercially and purchased (usually by individuals with no right to bear arms) as curiosities and souvenirs. A medieval knight would also have hung his decorated shield in the hall, together with his lance, poleaxe, mace, sword etc.

A heraldic achievement or coat of arms comprises a shield supported (often by two fabulous beasts), a helmet surmounted by a crest and surrounded by the elaborate drapery of the lambrequin, and a motto. Arms assumed by individuals became as much a part of the family heritage as the surname. Servants wore a livery of the family colours; a gentleman sealed his letters with the family arms; and the family napery was embroidered with a motto derived from a medieval warcry.

The possession of arms is supervised by the pursuivants,

heralds and kings of arms, incorporated (1484) in the College of Arms for England and Wales. Heraldry in Scotland is the province of the Lyon King of Arms.

Why a medieval warrior chose for his arms certain combinations of colours (gules, vert, sable, purpure, azure), metals (argent, or) and furs (ermines, ermine, erminois, vair) is not always known. Nor can the historian always be certain of the significance of the shield's charges (with griffins or savages, mullets or mitres, chevrons or lozenges). The language of heraldry is Norman-French. A coat of arms may include canting references to surnames; allusions to the personal qualities of an individual or the circumstances and origins of the family; and the impaling and quartering of two or more shields to show marriage alliances and other associations:

> 'quarterly, 1 and 4, argent on a chevron vert, between three wolves passant reguardant sable armed and langued gules, as many Lacy knots of the field (for De Lacy); 2 and 3, azure, crusily fitchy two dolphins hauriant embowed and addorsed or, within a bordure engrailed of the second (for Fitzgerald).'

Published armories and the manuscript collections of the colleges of arms and British Library will identify the families and surnames associated with each coat of arms.

Biography and directories

Biographical dictionaries (for instance, the *Dictionary of National Biography*) may contain brief details of an ancestor's career and achievements.

Directories of army and naval officers, clergy, surgeons, physicians, university graduates, architects, lawyers, engineers etc, commencing in the eighteenth century, give the name, address and qualifications of the professional classes. Commercial directories, listing householders, merchants, craftsmen, farmers, local officials etc, have been published for London since 1677 and the provinces since about 1780. Many directories also provide a topographical or historical sketch of the locality, which helps to place an ancestor in his proper setting.

Surnames

The study of surnames — their origin and meaning — may provide the family with significant clues to an ancestor's place of origin, social class, occupation, nationality, etc. Surnames were generally adopted as a means of distinguishing people of the same personal name. A surname often exists in a variety of different spellings, and indexes must therefore be searched very carefully: for example, the surname Garnet can be spelled

Warnett; and Garrett, Jarritt, Gerrad, Gerald, Jerrold, Garard and Jerrard may be used interchangeably.

A surname could be adopted by a landowner from the name of his village or estate: the Fitzhardinges of Bristol, moneylenders to Henry II, were rewarded with the estate of Berkeley — which became the family surname. However, most surnames of place indicate a district or town from which an individual or family migrated: Richard Poleworth, 1231; Richard of Fulham, 1269; William of Boresworth, 1290; William of Jarponville, 1323. Many Norman surnames originate in French place-names — Quincy, Lacy, Montgomery, Curzon, Beaumont, Grenfell, Quinton — and these names still have genteel, or even aristocratic, connotations. Less easy to interpret are names derived from common place-names — Easton, Weston, Sutton, Newton; or topographical features — Atwood, Freak, Milne, Field, Green, Muir, Burns, Lee — which inform the researcher only that an ancestor lived near or worked in the wood, frith, mill, field, green, moor, stream or woodland clearing.

Surnames derived from occupations indicate the family's trade or office at the time of the general adoption of surnames in the middle ages — Carpenter, Turner, Baker, Sumpter (driver of a packhorse), Sumner (summoner of persons to appear in court), Summerskill (herdsman at the shieling), Hollister (female brothel-keeper).

Some surnames describe physical peculiarities of individuals — Gifford (bloated), Cruickshank (lame leg), Cumming (crooked); or family characteristics — Fair, Brown, Black, Long, Grant (tall), Rouse (red-haired); while other surnames may refer to moral attributes — Dove (peaceful), Smart (clever), Good, Proud, Gay, Gentle, Sweet. But some names are more enigmatic — Curtis (courteous or short-hose); or misleading to the unwary — Coward (cowherd). And many names must have been ironically applied — Short (for a tall man), Thynne (for a fat man), Bold (for a coward).

Surnames expressing relationship usually derive from the father's name (patronymic): King Harold, who was killed at Hastings in 1066, was surnamed Godwinson; other similar names are easily identified — Johnson, Williamson, Richardson — even when shortened to Jones, Wills, Richards. Surnames from women's names include Annett (from Agnes), Margitson (Margaret), Marriot (Mary), Babbs (Barbara), Mudd (Maud). These names do not necessarily indicate illegitimacy. Post-humous infants also often took the mother's name. Or a man or woman born on a saint's feast day might honour the saint when adopting a surname: Sissons for Saint Cecilia (22nd November). An individual might adopt either the father's Christian name or his surname. It is not possible to know therefore whether Joan Johns was perpetuating a family surname or was simply the daughter of John (the village blacksmith, miller, hayward, etc).

In Wales patronymics sometimes altered in each generation as late as the nineteenth century: William Jones's son, Evan, being known as Evan Williams(on); Evan's son, Harry, being Harry Evans(on); Harry's son, Thomas, being Thomas Harris(on); or Thomas might also be known as Thomas ap Harry (*ap* = son of), and contractions of *ap* names give such characteristically Welsh surnames as Parry (ap Harry), Bevan (ap Evan), etc.

Equivalents to son in the Scottish Gaelic are *Mac* or *Mc;* in Irish, *Mc* (son of) or *O* (descendant of); in Norman-French, *Fitz*.

A further development may be found in communities where a very few surnames are borne by a large number of only distantly related families. Individuals or families may adopt an additional name: perhaps derived from an occupation — Jones the milk, Evans the hearse; or a tee name (nickname) of less clear origin — William Smith 'Stripie', William Smith 'Wockie', William Smith 'Fling'.

Irish and Scottish Gaelic surnames are frequently anglicised: Ó Cinneide (ugly head) becomes O'Kennedy. Names may be translated: the Irish Macanghabhann (son of the blacksmith) becomes Smithson; the Scottish Maciain (son of Iain) becomes Johnson. Or a surname may be corrupted or abandoned in favour of a more or less homophonous Anglo-Saxon name: the Irish Ó Gormghaile (descendant of Gormghal) becoming Grimes (variously meaning fierce, masked, spectre, goblin, or associated with the Saxon god Woden).

Newspapers

Newspapers and periodicals contain notices of birth, marriage and death; bankruptcy, divorce and naturalisation proceedings; records of criminal or civil trials (often more informative than surviving court records); biographical details of servicemen; reports of accidents; and celebrations of achievements in education, sport, the arts etc. Obituaries seldom give a balanced view of the deceased but are always useful in outlining an individual's career as well as (sometimes) naming both his antecedents and survivors. Newspaper files may be consulted at the relevant newspaper office or in public libraries, local record offices and the national libraries.

Editions, indexes and calendars

Microfilms, indexes, photocopies and published editions of archival documents may be available in the public library. The family historian may find it more convenient to study the parish registers, wills, censuses etc in microform, in the reference library.

Catalogues (calendars) of archival documents, lists of sources and guides to the holdings of national and local record offices are also available on the library shelves.

National, regional and specialist record societies publish editions and catalogues of archival documents, for example: the Catholic Record Society — a census of Oxburgh Catholics, 1790-1804, a list of convicted recusants, 1671, a list of boys at Liège Academy, 1773-1791; the Lancashire and Cheshire Record Society — the Talbot deeds with a pedigree of the Domvilles of Brimstage and Oxton before 1400; the Historical Society of West Wales — genealogies of Cardiganshire, Carmarthenshire and Pembrokeshire families, Quaker emigrants to Pennsylvania.

During the late eighteenth and early nineteenth centuries there arose an increasing interest in historical studies, and commissioners were appointed to put in hand 'the better Arrangement, Preservation, and more convenient Use' of the public records, then 'perishing Daily by Damp in the Vaults . . . in extreme Confusion . . . exposed to the most imminent Risk of Destruction by Fire'. The record commissioners compiled and published extensive lists and calendars and identified 'those Documents which it is useless . . . to preserve'.

Local histories

The Victoria History of the Counties of England and detailed individual studies of boroughs or parishes provide background information on the development of towns, estates, industrial enterprises, trade, agriculture; economic and social conditions; and the activities of families and individuals responding to, and shaping, their environment.

Gazetteers (for example Groome's *Ordnance Gazetteer of Scotland,* 1882-6), describe the towns, cities, parishes, and villages of Britain — their history, population, agriculture, industry, markets, churches, fairs, utilities etc.

Maps and plans

Atlases of views and prospects, town plans, estate maps and Ordnance Survey plans may preserve an impression of the landscape or townscape an ancestor would have known, although the precise identification of the family home may not be very easy. Much of this visual material was printed for sale to the public: John Wood's plans of forty-eight Scottish towns, (1819-26) were drawn at large enough scales to show individual houses and names of property owners.

One-inch maps of England and Wales, the work of Board of Ordnance surveyors, began to be published in 1801. By the late nineteenth century the Ordnance Survey had published six-inch maps of the whole of Britain and twenty-five-inch maps of most of the country. The Ordnance Survey also published large-scale (up to 1:500) town plans, which clearly show the shape of every building with porches, bay windows, conservatories, outbuildings, privies, as well as the layout of gardens and grounds with orchards, trees, shrubberies, walks and ponds. However, names of people (unless added by a later hand) do not appear on Ordnance Survey plans, but by using maps in conjunction with census and valuation, an ancestor's property can often be identified.

Retracing an ancestor's steps from home to workplace, school or chapel can be a rewarding (and emotional) experience well worth recording on film or tape. Many streets and buildings may remain unaltered, and the people the searcher meets may be descendants of an ancestor's friends and workmates — or even distant relations — with tales to tell of the place and its inhabitants.

Societies

Joining the local history or antiquarian group opens to the genealogist the society's library and the works of its members.

Local family history societies provide valuable guidance for the beginner and are united in the Federation of Family History Societies, formed in 1974. The federation produces a variety of aids for the genealogist: blank pedigree charts; keys to indexes of the registration districts; family questionnaire forms; forms for census returns and for parish register searches; family group sheets; guides to census returns, bishops' transcripts, etc; handlists on the recording of family trees and monumental inscriptions; and registers of individuals and societies working in the field of genealogy. A Guild of One-Name Studies unites single-surname societies, which coordinate and assist the work of individuals researching the same surname.

The Society of Genealogists maintains, in London, a library of genealogical and heraldic books, periodicals, microfilms and microfiches. The collection also includes printed copies of parish registers, monumental inscriptions, indexes of wills and marriage licences; a documentary collection of pedigrees and notes on families; the International Genealogical Index (IGI); family histories; Boyd's index of marriages and of inhabitants of London; a 'great card index' referring to English surnames from a variety of sources; and the Bernau index to Chancery proceedings.

The Church of Jesus Christ of Latter-Day Saints (the Mormons) preserves microfilms of parish registers and other archives in the Granite Mountain records vault, Utah. Copies of these microfilms are available in public libraries and branch libraries of the Mormon church. The library of the genealogical department, Salt Lake City, provides a reference service for family historians, including the International Genealogical Index (IGI), the family group records archive and other indexes.

3. The record office

The genealogist should expect to spend many hours in the searchroom of the county record office, where the archives of quarter sessions, churches, estates, parishes, boroughs, lawyers, factories and private families are preserved for the use of historians, genealogists, etc. A few collections will be unavailable to researchers to protect the interests or privacy of their owners. Rules may vary but, generally, documents are restricted for thirty years, though more confidential material (medical records, some solicitors' archives) may be unavailable for one hundred years.

The archivist's first duty is to the documents deposited in the record office — to maintain their physical condition and archival integrity. And so searchers are not permitted to browse in the strongrooms where documents are stored, and stringent regulations and strict supervision are enforced in the searchroom.

Access to documents is through lists or catalogues (calendars) and card indexes of names, places and subjects — and by seeking the advice of the archivists.

The researcher is likely to find many documents written in Latin (the language of the law, church and government), and some early documents in Norman-French or in the Celtic vernaculars; but most will be in English — or in Middle English, or a variety of regional dialects.

But the handwriting of historical documents may (at first) make them unintelligible even to the most skilled linguist. Specialist tuition in palaeography is not always available locally, but by studying the examples in various textbooks and with practice (requesting the archivist's aid in the case of particular difficulties) most ancient scripts may be deciphered.

The medieval law courts and administrative departments (Exchequer, Chancery, King's Bench, etc) developed their own peculiar scripts. These were officially abandoned in 1733 in favour of 'a common legible Hand and Character', but many clerks continued writing in the old law hands until the nineteenth century. However, the formal scripts of royal charters, book hands employed in the copying of psalters, missals and literary works, and court hands are less likely to be a trouble to the genealogist than the current secretary hand of the sixteenth century (the script used for parish registers, local administration, and business, legal and family records). A carefully written secretary hand presents few difficulties but when hastily written the hand may be more difficult to decipher. Italic influences, discernible in sixteenth-century documents, became increasingly pervasive during the seventeenth century. Italic script replaced secretary during the eighteenth century, developing into an elegant cursive writing (much favoured by engravers, and so

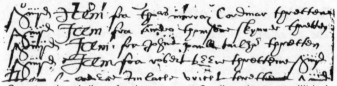

Secretary hand: 'item fra thoas murray Cordinar threttene s iiijd...'

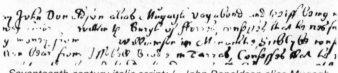

Seventeenth-century italic script: '...John Donaldson alias Mugagh vagabond and theiff...'

The copperplate script of a Victorian schoolboy.

known as copperplate) practised in the Victorian schoolboy's copy book.

The dating of historical documents may also present some slight difficulties to the beginner. In 1582 the calendar was reformed. The new year now began on 1st January instead of Lady Day (25th March). The new (Gregorian) calendar was used in Scotland from 1600, and in the remainder of Britain from 1752. But many writers continued using the old calendar though perhaps adopting 1st January as the beginning of the year:

> M[arch] 30 [1690] the Lord's day . . . testified
> . . . fully ag[ains]t the most of ye defections of
> Min[iste]rs & professours of ye wholl land
> . . . and supped in W[illia]m Edonis, qr I was
> kindlie intertained.

But 30th March was a Thursday by the new style calendar. The writer, James Allan, a minister and a careful diarist, was unlikely to make such an error. The difficulty is resolved by reference to printed calendars which show 30th March falling on a Sunday in 1690 according to the Julian (old style) calendar.

4. Family stories

Every member of the family has a tale to tell. The reminiscences of relatives should be collected and preserved, for the small anecdotes and significant episodes in an individual's life — secret hopes, fears and sadnesses — are often not recorded in documentary sources. An elderly relative, telling a tale learned as a child at his own grandfather's knee, spans a century or more of the family history. And younger relatives, parents, aunts and uncles, will add significant (and sometimes surprising or contradictory) details to the family story: family jokes, secrets, legends; as well as descriptions of living and dead individuals — peculiarities of temper, mannerism, taste, ability, humour, attitude and opinion — learned from both personal experience and hearsay.

But human memory is fallible. An aged relative may not have been listening very attentively when her own grandfather related the episodes of his youth — and certainly was not thinking of the value of such facts to family historians of the future. And the process of remembering is sometimes more creative than truthful as the ignorant or forgetful informant conjures from imagination the facts which the questioner seems anxious to hear.

The basic facts of a family legend (perhaps preserved only orally through several generations) are likely to be thickly encrusted with the imaginative embellishments of each retelling. The skilful interviewer must therefore learn to detect the threads of fact in the embroidery of fiction and to know when, through some affected niceness, an episode of illegitimacy, divorce, crime, poverty, etc, is being avoided or concealed.

For recording interviews a portable cassette-recorder preserves the maximum information with the least trouble and expense. Shorthand notes cannot keep pace with the flow of reminiscences which come from the more enthusiastic informants. Nor can written notes reproduce an individual's quirks of emphasis and inflexion. Video, while doubtless preserving the most complete record, is an expensive medium, and one which requires of the interviewer much skill if the interviewee is to be set at ease.

The first task of the interviewer (and perhaps the hardest) is helping the interviewee to relax: a comfortable chair and a warm fire in the subject's own living room; a glass of sherry to lubricate the vocal chords; a family album to start the memories flowing. Some interviewees will be old, frail in body and weak in mind; many will be shy or tedious; others will be downright obstructive, even rude, or deliberately enigmatic, malicious, vindictive. They may tell lies. Most informants will be unused to severe questioning and unlikely to recall incidents as accurately or to date them as precisely as the genealogist might wish.

Questions must be carefully framed. Questions must be suited to the interviewee's personality and intellect — comprehensible but not patronising, penetrating but not impertinent. The interviewee may choose to speak frankly, in which case the interviewer must be prepared to listen patiently, without appearing shocked or embarrassed by, or critical of, any revelation which may be made, and not betraying impatience if the subject strays from the strict confines of the family history. But the tape should never be edited. The significance of an apparent irrelevance may be shown later, and all of a relative's thoughts and words are useful as indicative of character and attitude. However, the interviewee may absolutely refuse to discuss such personal or painful subjects as sex, death, divorce, crime or wartime experiences, and the interviewer must respect the limits defined by the informant and seek some safer avenue of enquiry.

The interviewer must be perfectly familiar with his equipment. The recorder must be in good working order, able to be set up without fuss or delay. Microphones must be placed appropriately to pick up the words of both interviewer and subject — but unobtrusively. And the interviewer can hardly expect the subject to supply adaptors, fuses, extension leads, spare tapes and batteries.

At the beginning of each tape should be recorded the names of interviewer and interviewee, and the subject, place and date of the conversation. This information should also appear on the outside of the cassette and cassette box. And, while the conversation is still fresh in the family historian's own memory, the tape should be accurately transcribed and typed. The typescript may be annotated to reproduce nuances of emphasis and inflexion and should be carefully checked for any inconsistencies of place or time which the account may contain. Such ambiguities may be resolved during a second session. A typed synopsis of each transcribed tape may prove useful when collating and analysing the facts revealed.

A structured interview requires the preparation in advance of a questionnaire. Questions asked in logical sequence (chronologically is to be preferred) provide the maximum information, making the most of the opportunity — perhaps the last opportunity — of speaking with an aged relative. But the structure should never be so rigid or pervasive as to make the conversation impersonal and the interviewee uncomfortable; nor should the structure be so pedantically adhered to as to prevent digression into more interesting, unforeseen areas.

A STRUCTURED QUESTIONNAIRE

Childhood
- date and place of birth
- parentage, brothers and sisters
- earliest memory
- unpleasant episodes: death, illness, accident, scandals
- pleasant episodes: holidays, birthdays, Christmas, trips and treats
- home: address, description, contents, garden, street
- religion: Sunday school
- hobbies and pastimes, fashions and fads, games
- food and clothing
- school: subjects, interests, awards, friends, teachers, pranks and punishment
- youth groups
- girlfriends, boyfriends, first date, first love, sex

Young adult
- college: subjects (why chosen), awards, friends (social status, etc), teachers, sports, societies, politics
- voluntary service
- military service: stations, combat, rank, exploits, discipline, comrades, officers
- apprenticeship and other training

Career
- childhood ambitions
- jobs: dates, firms, types of work, wages, promotions, colleagues, bosses, working conditions, travel, accidents
- trade union: membership, office, strikes
- retirement

Marriage
- fiancés, love affairs and liaisons
- homosexuality
- spouse: first impression, subsequent impression, developing relationship
- in-laws: first impression, subsequent relationship
- proposal
- wedding: place, guests, speeches, finances, reception
- honeymoon
- adultery
- divorce

Family
>children: names, birthdays, character, first words, hobbies, schools
>daily routine: food, clothes, home comforts
>activities: games, walks, charades, trips
>holidays

Community involvement
>church: denomination, offices
>politics: membership of party, offices
>friends
>enemies
>neighbours
>clubs and societies
>culture: arts, theatre, amateur dramatics

Personality
>religion: views on God, life, death
>politics: views on class, economics, race, ecology
>health
>prosperity: good times, bad times, achievements, disappointments
>aspirations

5. Family papers

Every family creates a large quantity of paperwork — bills, letters, old ration books, school books, certificates, photographs. But seldom are such collections recognised as muniments and even more rarely is the archive preserved for posterity. The documents contained in the suitcase on top of the wardrobe or under the bed, the papers in the box in the attic or in the sideboard should be thoroughly sifted by the historian. The family archive is likely to contain several birth, marriage or death certificates, saving the researcher the time, trouble and expense of a visit to the registrar. And many other official documents may be preserved — lair certificates, rate demands, national insurance cards, post office savings books, passports, tax returns and codings. Official archives may duplicate these sources, though certain 'particular instance papers' are destroyed, and with them much of an individual's personal history.

Diplomas, degrees, certificates, citations and medals are awarded as proof of competence, achievement or conspicuous service in the course of education, professional training and military service. School reports, exercise books, examination papers, lecture notes, prize books and leaving certificates are informative but rare documents seldom preserved even in official archives.

Family correspondence (letters, telegrams, memoranda, post-cards, Christmas cards) reveals aspects of family history — the personality of the writer, attitudes to events of the day, personal finances, marital problems and employment prospects, the commonplace and the exceptional.

It is possible that an individual with genealogical instincts has already recorded events relating to the family in birthday books, autograph albums or scrapbooks containing photographs, news-paper cuttings, signatures and drawings — or perhaps a pedigree already exists.

A heavy folio Bible, an old prayer book or perhaps a finely bound uncut Victorian copy of *Pilgrim's Progress* or *Paradise Lost* may grace or clutter a bookshelf somewhere in the house. Such volumes may have been handed down through several generations and the endpapers used to record births, marriages and deaths in the family — but such information should always be confirmed in official sources:

> Alfred Cogger And Margaret Watson Was Mared On the 15th Day of Aprial 1857 this Boock Was Made A present to Me ... by My Mother Elizabeth Cogger ... Charles James Cogger Was lost in the Schoonar Viscount McDuff ... on a Voige from Sidney to ... bay of Bengall ... 1882

Once an individual begins to keep a daily journal — of secret thoughts and personal experiences, private conversations, crises, delights and disasters — it may become a lifelong obsession. But diaries are rare sources. Indeed, the well meaning executor is more likely to preserve a useless printed pocket-book (listing train times and dental appointments) than the scruffy notebooks or the many reams of hastily written scrawl recording a man or woman's inner life.

No family can honestly claim never to have been involved with the law or the courts — or if so, family papers may prove otherwise. Debts and divorces, or criminal cases (theft, vandal-ism, illegal parking, dangerous driving, drunkenness) may be evidenced, and if such goings-on offend the genealogist he had better abandon his pursuit. For the black sheep tend to be by far the best documented — and most interesting — characters in the pedigree.

Visual (and audio) documentation — photographs, magnetic tapes, gramophone records, portraits, prints, sketches, home movies and videos — may tell more about an individual than any other single source: features and expressions, smiles, frowns, build, dress, mannerisms and environment; the way the subjects of a photograph are grouped (are the spouses holding hands?); the accidental capture on film of an angry glance. Copies of photographs from the family album should be included in the relevant individual's file, and the pedigree can be brought to life by mounting it with a small portrait of each ancestor.

The conservationist at the local record office should be consulted for specialist advice on the copying, storage and display of original prints and negatives, and the archivist will always be pleased to examine and discuss collections of family papers, advise on conservation and storage, or accept the collection on loan or as a gift for permanent preservation in the record office. Some visual material and artefacts — sculptures, sketches, portraits, samplers, pottery — may give a telling insight into the taste and craftsmanship of past generations.

The urge to write is very strong in many (particularly middle-class) people, and family papers often include a small bundle of cheap notebooks or a ream of typescript containing the manuscript of a novel, a collection of adolescent verse, or autobiographical notes and memoirs. Such texts, however naive or pretentious, may, by their very crudeness, be more revealing of an ancestor's personality than the detached, polished work of a professional writer. Published books and articles are, however, a valuable source for family history, revealing, perhaps, an ancestor's social and political prejudices. But collections of drafts and notes may reveal far more — sentiments too idiosyncratic or too outrageous to be accepted by the publisher.

Bundles of bills and receipts reveal a family's way of life — and death:

> March 13 To a full mounted coffin in embossed velvet (for Martha Jane Cruickshank Aged 8½ months) with nickel plated mounting, ropes & silk tassels, inside lined with best rubber macintosh ... £2 7s 6d ... Paid Phimister for landau & pair 15s 0d [1905]

Obituary notices, memorial cards, letters of condolence and messages accompanying floral tributes usefully (if seldom entirely honestly) sum up an individual's career. Perhaps a more intimate relic of an ancestor may survive: a lock of hair in a brooch; some specimen of Victorian mawkishness such as a plaster cast of an infant's hand or foot; a baby's tooth 'left for the fairies'; a death mask; an urn of ashes on grandmother's mantelpiece.

The physical remains of only a very few people (Lenin, Jeremy Bentham, Tutankhamen, John Torrington) have been preserved for posterity. But it may not be impossible to see an ancestor's skeleton or skull. Medical institutions and museums often possess a collection of human bones — and every one belongs to someone's ancestor. It may be possible to put a name to these gruesome relics. If one's forebears did not donate their bodies to science, or experience 'resurrection' in the interests of science, the searcher himself may take a closer look into the local cemetery. For some soils have remarkable preservative properties — and there is nothing preventing any citizen from raising an action for disinterment with the sheriff or requesting an exhumation licence from the Home Office. A detailed scientific analysis of the bones or body may reveal aspects of an individual's medical history — diet, wounds, diseases, deformities, accidental injuries, and cause of death.

And the prescient family historian will not have missed the genealogical implications of cryogenics, cloning or sperm banks.

6. Civil registers

Civil registration of births, marriages and deaths began in England and Wales on 1st July 1837. Superintendent registrars were appointed to record the information locally and to issue birth, marriage and death certificates. A copy of each registration was despatched to the Registrar General in London, for inclusion in a duplicate register covering the whole of England and Wales. Copy certificates may be purchased, by post or in person, either from the Registrar General or locally at the office of the relevant superintendent registrar, who, for a fee, will search for a particular entry over a five-year period. The index to the national register in London may be consulted free of charge; however, some local registrars charge a fee to searchers. It is simpler to find a certificate from the national registers than locally, if the exact location is not known.

Civil registration began in Scotland in 1855; Ireland in 1864 (Protestant marriages from 1845); the Isle of Man in 1849 (marriages) and 1878 (births and deaths); Northern Ireland in 1922; Jersey in 1842; and the states of Guernsey in 1840 (Church of England marriages from 1919). Records for the whole of each region (except Jersey) are kept by a registrar general, and registers for each locality may be consulted at the office of the relevant registrar.

The details required to be recorded in the registers have varied over the years. Variations also occur between regions: Scottish certificates are, in some respects, more informative than others. However, the basic information recorded remains the same. A birth certificate shows the child's name, date and place of birth and parentage including the mother's maiden name and father's occupation.

Birth certificate

REGISTRATION DISTRICT   Newport
DOSBARTH COFRESTRU

1839 BIRTH in the Sub-district of   Saint Woolos in the County of Monmouth
Genedigaeth yn Is-ddosbarth

No. Rhif	When and where born Pryd a lie y ganwyd	Name if any Enw os oes un	Sex Rhyw	Name and surname of father Enw a chyfenw'r tad	Name, surname and maiden surname of mother Enw, cyfenw a chyfenw morwynol y fam	Occupation of father Gwaith y tad	Signature, description and residence of informant Llofnod disgrifiad a chyfeiriad yr hysbysydd	When registered Pryd y cofrestrwyd
199.	Seventh of February 1839. Hamlet of Graig, 8 A.M.	Herbert	Boy	Charles Mather.	Harriet Mather formerly Bennett.	Gardner.	Charles Mather Father Hamlet of Graig.	Twenty first of March 1839.

Birth certificate

Marriage certificate

1859 Marriage solemnized at the Parish Church in the Parish of Liverpool in the County of Lancaster

No.	When married.	Name and Surname.	Age.	Condition.	Rank or Profession.	Residence at the time of Marriage.	Father's Name and Surname.	Rank or Profession.
80	23rd August 1859	Horatio Mather	full	Bachelor	Victualler	College Lane	Charles Mather	Gardener
		Jane Roberts	full	Spinster		College Lane	William Roberts	Collier

Married in the Parish Church according to the Rites and Ceremonies of the Established Church. by or after Banns by me. A H Denny Curate

This Marriage was solemnized between us. { Horatio Mather Jane Roberts her x mark } in the presence of us. { William Jones Susannah Jones

Marriage certificate

24

Marriage certificates detail names, occupations and places of residence. In some cases though, instead of recording the exact ages of the parties, the registrar may note only that they are 'of full age'.

Death certificates are not always accurate. A death may be registered by a friend or neighbour able to provide only an approximate age. If the circumstances surrounding a death are suspicious or unusual a coroner's court will investigate. Various collections of coroners' inquests dating from the thirteenth century onwards are held at the Public Record Office and at some county record offices. However, a much more readily available and informative source for recent inquests will be the reports of coroners' proceedings in the local newspapers.

Most people die in their beds. The place of death is important as it may have been a family home for several generations and further information may be gleaned from census returns, or by visiting the neighbourhood and examining the sanitation, accommodation, fittings and décor of the house, and interviewing neighbours who may possess some memory or written record of the deceased.

The genealogist begins the investigation from a set of known facts — name, date and place — if necessary from his or her own birth certificate. From these known facts the searcher works backwards in time — into the unknown. A birth certificate records the names of parents and, using this information and the registrar's indexes, a marriage certificate should be located. Taking the names, ages and dates on the marriage certificate as a new starting point, the registrar's indexes lead the searcher to the parents' birth certificates — and so to the marriage of *their* parents.

Working in this manner, a pedigree can be traced back to early Victorian times, unless hampered by some irregularity in the family history. The registers do not record the relationship of couples who choose to live together as man and wife without a formal wedding. An ancestor who changed his or her surname other than on marriage may also be difficult to trace in the registers. And the birth certificates of illegitimate children often do not record the father's name, which must be sought in other records. Research in the male line may be temporarily brought to a halt, but the serious genealogist never ignores a female line of descent. And where the father of a child is unknown the role of the mother in the family history is doubly significant.

If a thorough search in the registers fails to reveal relevant information, the genealogist must search the several separate series of registers which record births, marriages and deaths occurring in particular unusual circumstances: registrations concerning military personnel and merchant seamen; marriages performed by ships' captains; births and deaths on the high seas

REGISTRATION DISTRICT	Birkenhead						

1886
DEATH in the Sub-District of *Birkenhead* in the *County of Chester*

When and Where died	Name and surname	Sex	Age	Occupation	Cause of death	Signature, description and residence of informant	When registered
Twenty seventh March 1886 97 Claughton Road	Charles Mather	Male	71 years	Gardener and domestic	Senile dementia 3 months Pneumonia Certified by G. R. Paterson M.D.	Emily Woosnam Granddaughter present at death 97 Claughton Road Birkenhead	Twenty seventh March 1886

Death certificate

26

or in foreign countries. The searcher may need to travel further afield in order to consult these and similar records. Some registers are kept by the Registrar General but others will be found at the Public Record Office, among Board of Trade records, or with the records accumulated at Llandaff by the Registrar General of Seamen and Shipping.

In addition to the basic facts of family life, the genealogist may encounter other, less usual events. Divorce in England before 1857 was achieved by promoting a private act of Parliament. Alternatively the ecclesiastical courts (Court of Arches, etc) might grant either a legal separation or dissolution of the marriage on grounds of consanguinity, impotency, pre-contract etc. From 1858 jurisdiction was exercised by a new court for divorce and matrimonial causes (later, the Family Division of the High Court of Justice). An act of Parliament of 1967 conferred jurisdiction in certain matrimonial proceedings on county courts. Divorce in Scotland fell under the jurisdiction of the commissary courts from 1563 to 1830, the Court of Session from 1830 to 1984, and the sheriff courts and Court of Session from 1984 onwards. Also in 1984 the General Register Office for Scotland established a central register of divorces. When a decree of divorce was granted an appropriate note was added in both the marriage and corrected entries registers. Files of correspondence concerning divorces will be preserved in the archives of the parties' solicitors. However, access to such collections is difficult and, even if the solicitors' accumulated papers are deposited on loan in a record office, files may be unavailable for fifty or even a hundred years.

Legal adoption has existed since 1927 in England and Wales (1930 in Scotland). Before this date many children were, for various reasons, not brought up by their natural parents, but records of the arrangements in these cases must be traced through family papers, school registers, poor law records, etc, rather than the Registrar General's indexes. The introduction of counselling for adoptees wishing to trace their natural parents is a recent innovation. For the genealogist, research is facilitated by the cross-indexing of birth and adoption certificates, the annotation of birth certificates, and the keeping of the adopted children register.

Registers of baptism, marriage and burial for the established (Presbyterian) church in Scotland from the sixteenth century onwards, are held at the General Register Office, Edinburgh, though microfilms may be available in public libraries etc.

Registers (mostly after 1634) for the Protestant Church of Ireland (disestablished in 1868) were deposited in the Public Record Office, Dublin, and destroyed in the fire of 1922. Volumes not deposited, and Roman Catholic registers, may survive locally or on microfilm in libraries, etc.

| ROAD, STREET, etc. and No. or NAME OF HOUSE | HOUSES | | NAME and Surname of each Person | RELATION to Head of Family | CON-DITION as to Marriage | AGE last Birthday of | | Rank, Profession, or OCCUPATION | WHERE BORN | (1) Deaf-and-Dumb (2) Blind (3) Imbecile or Idiot (4) Lunatic |
	In-habited	Unin-habited				Males	Females			
17 Millstone Lane	1		Sanders Quincey	Head	M	45		Mineral Water Manuf	Northampton-shire, Oundle	
			Elizabeth do	Wife	do		44		Warwickshire, Coventry	
			Elizabeth Russell do	Daughter	Unm		21		Lancashire, Manchester	
			Sanders Herbert do	Son	do	19		Pianoforte Manuf	Warwickshire, Coventry	
			James do	Brother Visitor	M	47		Provision Dealer	Northampton-shire, Cotterstock	

Census return form

I G I MICROFICHE		PAGE 10,184						
COUNTRY : WALES							SOURCE	
NAME	FATHER/MOTHER OR SPOUSE	MALE FEMALE HUSBAND WIFE	CHRISTENING MARRIAGE	EVENT DATE	PARISH		BATCH	SERIAL SHEET
WOOSNAM, BOWEN	ELIZA COLE	M	M	25 JAN 1805	MONTGOMERY LLANIDLOES		7222025	92
WOOSNAM, CHARLES	EVAN WOOSNAM/ ELIZABETH GEORGE	M	C	21 MAY 1833	MONTGOMERY LLANIDLOES		7222025	39

International Genealogical Index microfiche

7. Census

The family historian, having traced all possible forebears in the registrar's records, should next turn to the census, which will begin to fill out the bare details of the Victorian ancestors' lives.

Lists of inhabitants, compiled by various officials from medieval times onwards, may be consulted in local and national archives. However, the specific administrative purposes which such lists served seldom required the naming of every man, woman and child in the parish. A census does survive for the parish of Ealing in 1599, and for the baronies of Newcastle and Upper Cross, County Dublin, about 1652; but these, and a handful of other local lists compiled before the end of the seventeenth century, are rare exceptions.

In 1753 a bill 'for taking an Account of the Population of Great Britain' — a national census — was rejected by Parliament. Suspicions that the census might be used by government to tax the people more effectively were probably not ill founded. The Scottish population surveys (Webster, 1755, and the first statistical account, 1790) are not genealogically useful.

In 1801 the government, finding it 'expedient to take an account of the total Number of Persons within the Kingdom of Great Britain', instigated the first national census, and, since 1801, a census has been taken every ten years (except 1941). The type of information that each householder is required to supply to the enumerator has not changed very markedly from 1841 to the present day.

From 1801 to 1831 the government was concerned with statistics — to measure 'the progressive Increase or Diminution of the population', in order to facilitate economic planning; and only occasionally, and by chance, have written returns survived from the first four censuses (1801-31). From 1841 onwards, the detailed returns have been preserved for posterity at the public record offices in London and Edinburgh. The collections are sealed for one hundred years to preserve confidentiality, after which time they are available for research. Searchers may also purchase copies or, perhaps more conveniently, study the census on microfilm in local libraries and record offices.

The returns, handwritten on printed forms, are arranged by county, town and parish. Every house (whether inhabited or not) is separately noticed, and, where appropriate, the different households living in each building are separately recorded. Every member of the household is mentioned, including servants, lodgers and (theoretically) any visitors staying in the house on census night.

The Irish situation is somewhat confused and confusing: the first census of Ireland was taken in 1813, and a census has been organised at intervals variously of five, eight and ten years. This need not trouble the researcher too much as it was government policy to destroy the returns for 1861-91 and those of 1841-51 were lost in the civil war of 1922; however, the returns for 1901 and 1911 are publicly available.

8. Parish records

The registration of baptisms, marriages and burials in England and Wales began in 1538 on the orders of Thomas Cromwell, chief minister to Henry VIII. Cromwell's mandate, while instructing parish clergy to provide secure storage for the registers, did not specify with any precision the information to be recorded, and until 1753 and 1812, when standard forms were introduced, the content of register entries varied considerably. A baptismal registration might contain only the most meagre information:

Jn Oldefeild bapt 11 Apr 1613

Other registrations contain miniature genealogies, detailing the names, residences and occupations not only of a child's parents, but of the grandparents too.

Few burial entries record the deceased's age: 'Mary Jardin bur 17 March 1686' might be an infant or a centenarian. And entries registering the burial of travelling folk, beggars, paupers or other strangers dying in the parish might not even contain a name. However parish priests were not averse to sycophantic prolixity when occasion demanded. To commemorate the passing of a local magnate or a wealthy benefactor the priest might use the register to preserve for posterity a record of the deceased's life and benevolence. The inclusion of aliases or nicknames may be helpful to the genealogist: 'James Smith, known as Black Jack'; while other additional information may be somewhat enigmatic: 'John Jones ancient Britoner'.

But many people suspected the government's motives and Cromwell's injunctions were not, at first, generally observed. In 1597 a provincial constitution of Canterbury obliged the clergy to keep registers on parchment rather than paper and to copy any earlier registers into the new volumes. This introduction particularly mentioned registrations made since the accession of Elizabeth I. Many clerks mistook this suggestion for an order and ignored entries prior to 1558; consequently registers dating back to 1538 are not common.

From 1597 the parish clergy were also required, each year, to transmit a copy of the registers to the diocesan authorities. Known as bishop's transcripts, these documents sometimes give more detail than the parish registers, but they may possibly also contain errors of transcription.

Many registers were not kept up during the Civil War and Commonwealth (1642-60) and, with the abolition of bishops, bishop's transcripts also ceased for a time. Registration resumed at the Restoration. From 1678 the word *affidavit* appearing in a burial register indicates that the relatives of the deceased have affirmed their compliance with the Act of Parliament requiring corpses to be buried 'in wool' (in woollen shrouds). This means of supporting England's textile industry was officially abandoned in 1814. Under an Act of 1694 duties were levied on parochial registrations of 'Persons married, buried, christened or born', and on bachelors and childless widowers, 'for the Term of five Years'. The duty proved almost impossible to collect. Exchequer returns are missing but local lists may be preserved in the parish chest. Between 1783 and 1794 a second attempt to raise money from register entries (paupers excepted) was no more successful. The number of registered 'paupers' increased, while other people did not bother baptising their children.

From the seventeenth century onwards, in the environs of London prisons, in marriage shops and chapels such as St James's, Duke's Place, and at remote churches such as Peak Forest, Derbyshire, it was possible for a man and woman to marry, secure from prying eyes and without the trouble and expense of banns and licences. The eighteenth century saw an epidemic of clandestine marriage. If nobody enquired too closely into the parson's qualifications he would not question the couple regarding their ages or motives. Some clandestine marriages were the result of elopements — genuine love matches; but there are also many stories of gullible young men being duped into marriage with Drury Lane 'actresses', or naive heiresses being seduced or abducted to be married under duress to penniless adventurers. The officiating clergymen could earn a good living from the trade.

The genealogist who unearths the record of a clandestine marriage will justifiably suspect that some forgotten family scandal or tragedy has occurred. But the facts can be discovered only in a few cases — and then only by a careful search for other sources. If no evidence survives, in family muniments or in later litigation in the commissary court, the researcher must be content with a tantalising register entry — and his own private speculations. Registers of clandestine marriages spanning at least the period 1667-1777 are held at the Public Record Office and in certain county record offices.

The 'great Mischiefs and Inconveniences' arising from clandestine marriages were remedied by Hardwicke's Marriage Act of 1753. The new law applied to all marriages except those of Jews and Quakers and in Scotland, where marriage by cohabitation and repute was recognised until 1939. Indeed, Hardwicke's

Act had the effect of reversing the direction of flow of elopements. Couples now headed not to London, but north to the Scottish border to Lamberton tollbar or Gretna Green. Under the Act marriages had to be performed in a parish church, following banns or licence, recorded in special registers on standard forms, signed by the officiating minister, bride, bridegroom and two witnesses.

Isaac Woosnam of *this* Parish
Painter
and *Mary Ann Richardson* of *this* Parish
Spinster
were married in this *Chapel* by *Banns* with Consent of
this *second* Day of
October in the Year One thousand eight hundred and *twenty six*
By me *John Pulford BD Curate*
This Marriage was solemnised between us   *Isaac Woosnam*
                                    Mary Ann Richardson
                                    x her mark
In the Presence of   *Edward Lovatt*
                    Ambrose Place
No. *685*

Printed standard forms were introduced for baptisms and burials on 1st January 1813.

Local registers are available on microfilm in public libraries, record offices, etc. Other microfilmed registers are obtainable from the Church of Jesus Christ of Latter-Day Saints (the Mormons). Some have been transcribed for publication by record societies.

Percival Boyd's indexes of English marriages, 1538-1837, and London burials, 1538-1853, are available at the Society of Genealogists. However, the International Genealogical Index (IGI) is probably the most exciting and ambitious family history project ever undertaken. Planned, financed and executed by the Church of Jesus Christ of Latter-Day Saints, this microfiche index contains many millions of entries, arranged by country, county, surname, Christian name and date. The names have been collected worldwide from parish registers, census returns, family pedigrees and other records, though with an emphasis upon the more genealogically productive events, for example baptisms (or births) and marriages — rather than burials (or deaths).

But the IGI is not absolutely reliable and the sources should always be double checked. Despite errors however, the index has revolutionised genealogical research, saving years of study and much tiresome travelling to record offices and churches. The IGI can be consulted in branch libraries of the Church of Jesus Christ of Latter-Day Saints, public libraries, family history societies and county record offices.

The proclamation of banns had been required since 1216 and

the practice survived the Reformation to be included in the Book of Common Prayer. Hardwicke's Act stated that banns 'be published in an audible manner in the Parish Church . . . upon three *Sundays* preceding the Solemnization of Marriage'. The register indicates the intended place of marriage.

A licence to wed might be obtained from the bishop. This survives only rarely — in family muniments — but could be granted, according to canons of 1604, 'upon good caution and security taken'. This required a bond by two cautioners that no pre-contract or consanguinity existed as impediment as well as an affidavit or allegation by those obtaining the licence as to the age of the couple, their marital condition, parish of residence, church of proposed marriage, and consent of parents if necessary. These two documents were preserved in diocesan registry files and details entered in a register.

From medieval times onwards parish priests had the right to claim a tithe (one-tenth) of annual agricultural produce. Tithes in kind were commuted into fixed rent-charges under an Act of 1836. The large-scale plans and surveys of parishes, drawn to facilitate apportionment of money payments, can be used in conjunction with census returns to locate the houses, lands and industrial premises owned or occupied by parishioners. Tithe records are deposited in parish chests, county record offices or the Public Record Office.

Diocesan records include court and cause papers (Doctors Commons, etc), bishops' registers, files and benefice papers from the early thirteenth century to the present day. These documents refer to institutions of clerks to benefices, ordinations, presentations, sequestrations after the resignation or incapacity of the incumbent, clerical discipline, matrimonial causes, probate, tithes, visitations of parishes, examinations of schoolmasters and religious recusants, with licences to surgeons, midwives, curates and clerks.

Diocesan records are deposited in county record offices, and archdiocesan records at Lambeth Palace, London, or the Borthwick Institute, York. Parish records may remain at the parish church, though many have been deposited in county record offices.

Monumental inscriptions on gravestones and tombs and memorials on the walls of the church preserve genealogical information not often recorded elsewhere. But although panegyrics on the virtues and moral qualities of the deceased are often hardly credible and never to be entirely trusted, descriptions of a man's ancestry, career, family, descendants and cause of death are likely to be more or less accurately recorded. A memorial in stone or wood, perhaps inlaid and painted, may give a rare impression of the physical appearance of an ancestor — although the likeness may owe more to the deference paid by the sculptor to the deceased's memory and family than to any strict regard for truth.

Tombs of kings and queens, nobles, knights and clerics survive from medieval times. Tombs and memorials to members of the gentry, professional men, merchants, soldiers and parish clergymen become common from the sixteenth century.

From the thirteenth century to the seventeenth century members of the gentry, clergy and merchant class are commemorated in monumental brasses. The metal (known as latten, an alloy of copper and zinc) is countersunk into a stone slab and fixed with rivets or black pitch. On the surface of the latten, a representation of the deceased, clad in the most up-to-date armour or dressed in his or her finest gown, is engraved or carved in semi-relief. But the engravings on these memorials are not attempts at portraiture and only occasionally are the brasses personalised. But, whether the memorial be an elegant sculpture or a simply incised slab, churchyard monuments provide the family historian with valuable evidence of the status, wealth and taste of the individuals and families for whom they were fashioned, and of the times in which they lived. An ancestor's actions may also be recorded in the name of the hospital or almshouse he founded, which may still stand in the parish as a testimony to his generosity.

Archives of congregations dissenting from the established church — Scottish Episcopalians, Congregationalists, Baptists, Religious Society of Friends (Quakers), Huguenots, Jews, Roman Catholics, Unitarians, Methodists, etc — include registers of baptism, marriage and burial, minutes of society meetings, school records, title deeds, charity papers, membership rolls, records of sufferings and financial accounts.

The central records of each denomination may be held at the sect's administrative headquarters. For some churches, records of individual congregations are centralised in a national archive. But the congregational records of other sects must be sought locally — at the relevant church, chapel, synagogue or meeting house — in university or public libraries and in county record offices.

Nine thousand volumes of nonconformist registers were deposited for authentication in the Public Record Office following the Registration Act of 1836. Microfilms of these are available in some public libraries and record offices, and details may be indexed on the IGI. The collection includes the extensive indexed registers of Bunhill Fields nonconformist burial ground, London, 1713-1838; also the nonconformist births registers maintained at Dr Williams's Library, London, 1742-1837. Unauthenticated registers (deposited since 1837) include Bethnal Green Gibraltar burial ground, 1793-1826. Records of the British Lying-in Hospital, Holborn, for distressed poor married women (especially the wives of soldiers and sailors), cover the period 1749 to 1868.

The Scottish kirk session, an influential parochial meeting representing an element of lay control over ecclesiastical affairs at congregational level, developed after the Reformation to superintend the moral, social and religious life of the community. The session consisted of the parish minister, elders and deacons, functioning under presbytery, synod and general assembly (with bishops until 1690) and in co-operation with town council, heritors (landowners) and justices of the peace. The session clerk often served as parochial schoolmaster and precentor; and the kirk supervised the education of children in parish and burgh schools. The session investigated complaints and punished offenders. Church door collections for the behoof of the poor were dispensed to persons listed on the roll and casual applicants. The session also acted as agents of the central government and from the pulpit were published the proclamations of civil and ecclesiastical authorities.

Records of the established church are deposited at the Scottish Record Office and in local record offices.

9. Wills

Even the least worldly of men is likely to be concerned about the disposition of his earthly goods after his death and so takes steps to make his will known regarding the property. The result of this concern is a document, often drawn up by a lawyer and expressed in the most unequivocal legal language, signed, dated and witnessed by those whom the testator considers most trustworthy.

A will, which deals with land, houses and other realty, or a testament, which disposes of goods and chattels (though technically only the testament was legal in England and Wales before the statute of wills in 1540), may be a calligraphic masterpiece written on parchment or a scrawled note on the back of an envelope. However, where a lawyer has been involved, the document tends to follow a standard pattern, beginning with an invocation — 'In the name of God, amen' — and continuing with the testator's name, occupation and place of residence with names of executors, followed perhaps by a note of the intended place of burial.

The property may be inherited by a single beneficiary or

disposed of piecemeal among a number of specified individuals.
Sometimes the testator records something of his feelings towards
his surviving relatives, or perhaps the imaginative genealogist
may perceive some hint as to family relationships:

> [and to] the most abandoned and deliberately
> infamous Wife that ever distinguished the annals
> of turpitude, as proved by her letters and conduct
> to me . . . should she be reduced to distress, and
> become really penitent . . . [1807]

To ensure further that the testator's wishes were carried out,
the will was usually proved in the court of the archdeacon or
bishop, or, less commonly, in the Court of Hustings in London,
other secular courts or testamentary peculiars. The Prerogative
Court of the Archbishop of Canterbury exercised testamentary
jurisdiction over England and Wales, proving the wills of men of
substance wherever resident and of those who died abroad or at
sea.

The executor was bound to keep proper accounts. Neighbours
were appointed to list the deceased's possessions. The appraisers
moved through the house and, room by room — 'in the chamber
over the Parlour . . . in the Kitchin . . . in the yellow Roome
. . .' — they listed kitchen utensils, bedding, clothing, stocks of
food, books, beasts, farm implements, tools and workshop or
warehouse contents. These documents were lodged with the
relevant ecclesiastical official, who recorded the process in his
probate act book and also sometimes registered a copy of the will
itself. This done, the executor received a probate copy of the
will. Diocesan act books also record the names of administra-
tors, curators and tutors appointed in cases of intestacy,
incompetence and minority.

Probate records of the Prerogative Court of Canterbury may
be consulted at the Public Record Office; of the Prerogative
Court of York at the Borthwick Institute, York; of other
jurisdictions at various county record offices and libraries. Welsh
wills are at the National Library of Wales.

In 1858 responsibility for proving and recording wills was
transferred to a newly established principal probate registry at
Somerset House, London, and to district registries throughout
England and Wales.

In Scotland, commissary courts replaced the medieval diocesan organisation in 1563, granting confirmation of testaments
and exercising jurisdiction in districts corresponding to medieval
bishoprics. Transcriptions of wills submitted for registration are
preserved in the commissary books. In cases of an individual
dying without making a will (intestate), the commissary nomin-
ated an executor for a testament dative. Testaments were
accompanied by inventories of the deceased's goods, gear,
money, debts, etc. Commissary records are indexed down to

1823 when sheriffs were appointed commissaries. From 1876 annual printed calendars have been published listing alphabetically confirmations and inventories granted in Scotland. Scottish probate records should be sought in the Scottish Record Office, Edinburgh, though the printed calendars may be available locally.

Problems may be experienced in finding the will of an Irish ancestor: following the establishment in 1858 of a principal registry in Dublin, and district registries, earlier probate records were deposited in the Public Record Office of Ireland but most were destroyed in the fire of 1922. However, wills dating from about 1900 onwards, volumes of copy wills (the earliest dated 1664-84), grant books (earliest 1684-8) and genealogical abstracts prepared by Sir William Betham, Ulster King of Arms, of prerogative wills to 1799, all furnish some evidence.

Probate records provide a vital key for the family historian, unlocking the door of an ancestor's home to reveal a long-vanished lifestyle: the comforts of the parlour; the conveniences of the kitchen; clothing and furniture; the taste of the individual and his age in the books on his shelf and the prints on his drawing room or library wall. The 'awls and naugers' or stock in trade of a craftsman will be listed in an inventory and examples of contemporary tools may be examined — or even handled — in the local museum.

Some families, however, did not bother with the troublesome probate procedure. This imprudence often gave disappointed relatives and would-be beneficiaries grounds for contesting the will. In some cases though, for instance where the existence of only one heir made a disputed succession improbable, the testator might safely dispense with the expensive security of probate. Copies of unproven wills must be sought among family muniments, many of which may be preserved in the nearly impenetrable confidentiality of a family solicitor's office.

10. Justice of the peace

From the fourteenth century justices of the peace assembled in the shires for administrative and judicial sessions. Firmly established in England and Wales as an important element of county government by the beginning of the seventeenth century, the justices met in petty or summary sessions, which might be called at any convenient location from the magistrate's own house to the local inn, and four times a year in formal courts of quarter sessions. Usually members of the gentry, local magnates, the justices were qualified by their social status rather than by any academic training. At each court of quarter session, therefore, they were advised by a clerk of the peace, typically a lawyer, who minuted the justices' deliberations. The clerk drew up schedules of proceedings from the various documents submitted to the court — presentments, indictments, petitions, etc — and was, in practice, responsible for the safe custody of the court's archives — session rolls, order books, etc. These records are available in county record offices, but minute and order books of summary or petty sessions rarely survive from before administrative reforms of 1828.

In Scotland 'godlie wyse and vertuous gentilmen of good qualitie' were annually appointed justices from 1609 in imitation of the English system; however, the courts did not achieve the same pre-eminence in local affairs. Some series of records are being transferred from the Scottish Record Office to local record offices.

At quarter and petty sessions the justices were empowered to 'ouersie, trye and prevent all sic occasionis as may breid truble ... and breach of [the] peace' — cases of assault, theft, trespass, riot, debt, nonpayment of rent, cattle stealing, witchcraft, drunkenness, refusal to continue in domestic service — but not cases of murder, treason, bigamy, etc. They received presentments, often from the constables who were responsible for maintaining law and order, and considered depositions and allegations:

> one George Foxe hath beene lately in these parts and hath uttered seuerall blasphemies [1652]

Presentment might lead to indictment:

> ag[ains]t William Athey of Harrold Butcher for that being Constable he spake these word[es], I care not a fart for any Justice of the peace in England [1658]

The justices considered evidence, questioned suspects and heard the statements of witnesses, sentencing the guilty to one or more of a variety of punishments — fines, flogging, imprisonment, mutilation, or exposure in the stocks, jougs or pillory:

> his hands to be tyed behind his back and a Label put on his breast with these words in Capital Letters A Notorious Thief and then to be brought from the Prison to the market Cross of Forres where he is to be put in the Joggs ... and thereafter to be drummed thro' the Town of Forres with a Sheaf of Corn & Straw upon his back, to which Burgh ... he is never to return [1773]

Another option was transportation: there are lists of criminals, political subversives and religious nonconformists shipped to the American plantations as indentured servants during the seventeenth century. However, most transportation records date from the early nineteenth century.

Petitions unconnected with crime were submitted to the court: poor relief, militia, aliment for debtors in prison, repair of highways, registration of nonconformist meeting houses, appointment to public office, etc.

From the sixteenth century an ever widening range of administrative duties was also imposed upon the justices. Few family historians will not have at least one ancestor recorded: contractors and labourers repairing roads and bridges; surveyors of parish highways; rate assessors; keepers, attendants and inmates in houses of correction, bridewells, jails and lunatic asylums; village constables.

The justices considered claims for relief in respect of families of militiamen posted elsewhere:

> I John Chisholm, a militia man serving in THE INVERNESS MILITIA do declare, That Elspet MacDonald [in LongBride] is my lawful wife, and has been so since the 10th day of Dec[embe]r. 1807. and that I have ... Two children ... Sophia aged 3 $\frac{4}{12}$, Hellen aged 2 years ... 11th day of January 1812

From 1662 onwards the justices administered the various laws of settlement and removal (of people likely to become a charge on the poor rate): itinerants, travelling folk, 'Egyptians', unemployed working men on tramp, unmarried mothers. Sessions records may contain the petition by a parish for the removal of a pauper; the judicial examination detailing the place of birth and marriage of a pauper, names of various towns in which he or she had lived and worked, age, usual occupation, names of spouse and children, and settlement; and the order for removal — Mary Flower, called before the justices at Richmond in 1815, having no legal settlement there, and being 'with Child of a bastard Child', was removed to Northallerton where her husband generously accepted the situation and baptised the child as his own son.

As the status and prestige of the court of quarter sessions increased, documents were deposited with the clerk of the peace for enrolment or registration. From 1536 deeds of bargain and sale of property were enrolled as a means of preventing fraud. The clerk recorded recognisances of good behaviour entered into, annually, by licensed victuallers under an act of 1552 (repealed 1828); and from 1563 itinerant sellers of corn, fish, cheese or butter (known as badgers) were licensed. Special licences were granted to victuallers on the military roads of Scotland. In 1797 James Gow or Smith (*gobha* = smith) was granted a licence to retail ale, beer or other British liquors free of duty at Bridgend of Dullnan, in 'a Decent regular Victualing house usefull for accomodating all foot Travellers as well as Military'. The inn lay near the river crossing on the strategic 'publick or Millitary Roadside' between Fort George and Inverness. Possibly James Gow's descendants, now known only as Smith, have forgotten their Gaelic roots.

Between 1662 and 1689 a tax of 2 shillings on every hearth was imposed on householders. Village constables served as chimney-men to compile lists of those liable (and sometimes of those exempt on grounds of poverty) for enrolment at the sessions, duplicates having been prepared for exchequer. From 1662 to 1674 individuals are named. The returns of 25th March 1664 are particularly complete. From 1673 onwards holders of public office were required to register oaths of loyalty to the king and established church. Between 1696 and 1832 constables returned lists of men with the necessary property qualification for jury service, showing each man's name, abode, age and occupation. The window tax was collected between 1696 and 1851. Annual returns arranged by parishes show the name and residence of the taxpayer with the number of windows in the house or business premises. Tyburn tickets — certificates of exemption from 'all Manner of Parish and Ward Offices' as reward for successfully bringing a felon to justice — were enrolled from 1699. Under an act of 1710 the lord of a manor registered the name of his gamekeeper. An act of 1715 compelled the registration of names of papists and descriptions of their real property; an act of 1717 necessitated the enrolment of their wills and deeds.

Copies of enclosure awards, agreements and plans were deposited for public consultation with the clerk of the peace and the relevant parish clerk. Land and labour could be exploited much more efficiently if, instead of working scattered strips in the open fields, a family consolidated its holdings into a compact farm of rectangular, hedged enclosures. By the careful manage-ment of the land and the acquisition by purchase or judicious marriage of adjacent farms and fields, a smallholding could become an estate entitling a peasant or yeoman to write 'gentleman' after his name and even to qualify for appointment as a county justice. But the process of enclosure could also result in a family being dispossessed of ancient but undocumented customary rights to cultivate strips in the arable, to graze cattle and sheep on the common muir, or gather firewood and feed pigs in the woodland. Such families might set up as craftsmen in the village or migrate to the towns, while many others became day labourers, working on the new farms of their sometime neighbours for board and wages.

In 1780 Parliament enacted that 'no Person shall vote for electing of ... Knights of the Shire to serve in Parliament ... which have not ... been charged or assessed ... by a Land Tax'. Until the parliamentary reform of 1832 returns of taxpayers within each parish were enrolled. Earlier returns, from 1692, may be found in family and estate papers. From 1832 registers of county voters were deposited. Until 1872, when the secret ballot was introduced, men's votes were recorded in poll books. Lists showing how each elector voted were often also reproduced in newspapers or printed for public display and sale. Under an act of 1711 'all the Poll Books' of a county election were to be deposited 'without any Imbezilment or Alteration'.

The clerk registered certificates issued to the owners of sporting dogs and guns under acts of 1784 and 1785. The court received returns of parochial charities under an act of 1786 and registered documents relating to charitable property from 1812.

Plans showing the route of proposed canals and inland navigations were required to be lodged, for public inspection, from 1792 onwards. A book of reference accompanied each plan identifying the owners and occupiers of land through which the cut was to run. Later, similar documentation for new roads, waterworks, land reclamation projects, railways, docks, gasworks and other public undertakings was lodged.

Users of hair powder paid a duty of one guinea annually from 1795 and the clerk registered the certificates of payment. From 1795 to 1871 the clerk maintained registers of the names of masters and owners of the larger boats and barges on inland navigations. Acts of 1795 and 1796 required a return from every township or parish listing men liable for service in the army and navy. Membership rolls of masonic lodges were enrolled annually under the Unlawful Societies Act of 1799. Some masons kept up their membership after migrating — to adjacent parishes, to industrial cities, or even abroad. The membership of the operative lodge of Rothes in 1809 includes:

William McKlean shepherd Abernethy
James Mcuilliam merchant Aberdeen

and the Forres St Lawrence lodge for 1817 includes:

John Hoyes Esq[uire] Grenada
Mr John Urquhart Merch[an]t Gibraltar
Captain A. B. Campbell Native Bombay
Inf[ant]r[y].

11. Estate muniments

Estate muniments record the history of the land, its owners and occupiers: tacksmen, farmers, cottars, domestic servants, etc; the churches and schools over which many landowners exerted considerable influence; the houses rented to labourers and tenants; and the mines, mills and other industrial enterprises in which rental income was invested.

The government in its various guises (National Coal Board, Crown Estates Commissioners, Ministry of Defence, Forestry Commission, etc) owns extensive estates, as do the church (ministers' glebes, city slums, lands gifted by pious benefactors), the universities (especially Oxford and Cambridge), private and public business firms, and families ranging from country squire or Scottish laird to aristocratic magnate.

The records may remain in the custody of the estate owner, perhaps preserved in a company head office or family muniment room; neglected in the attics and outbuildings of the big house; jealously guarded by a solicitor; or available to searchers, by appointment, in the estate office. But many estate collections are now deposited in public libraries and record offices.

The Historical Manuscripts Commission was appointed in 1869 to locate, list and index the wealth of family and estate muniments in Britain. The National Register of Archives commenced work in 1945 'to record the location, content and availability of all archives and collections of historical manuscripts ... other than records of the central government, without limit of date'. The register is supplemented by indexes of persons, places, etc.

The proprietor of a medieval landed estate in England or Wales (the lord of the manor) wielded considerable power within his domain, but he owed duties too. The fields, mill, moor, woods and waste were regulated by the manor court and by a variety of officials and villagers — hayward, woodward, cowherd, pinder, dykeman, hunter, miller, falconer, grieve, reeve, constable, sergeant, catchpoll and steward. Court rolls survive, for some manors, from the thirteenth century. Manorial jurisdiction was abolished in 1926.

The peasant farmer could surrender his lands only to his lord; and the lord admitted an heir or successor to a peasant's holding on payment of a customary fine. This process is recorded in manor court rolls while copies of the entries (surrenders and admittances) might be preserved as proof of title among the small archive of a peasant family. A bundle of such deeds may record many generations of a single family as lands pass from father to son.

A bundle of title deeds contains a variety of documents drawn up to identify the legal owners of property — medieval charters of grant; fines (agreements) in the courts securing a record of the conveyance of freehold; the feoffment to uses, evading burdensome feudal services; the bargain and sale from 1536; the lease and release from 1614 to 1841.

It is said that by the eighteenth century half the land in England was encumbered by strict legal settlements, which reflect the complexities of family relationships. A marriage settlement was drawn up to protect the interests of the individuals, families and properties concerned in the alliance. An estate might be settled jointly on husband and wife (jointure), the wife retaining the property even in widowhood, perhaps depriving the son of the enjoyment of the lands — giving the dowager a powerful position in the family. An entail limited the succession to an estate — perhaps excluding specified branches of the family — or might hinder or prevent the future division of the land or the development of the estate's resources. The entail might be broken through a collusive action of common recovery (a fifteenth-century device) or, from 1512, by an act of Parliament variously describing charges on the property, debts and dowries, remainders and reversions, and including a family pedigree.

A property may be mortgaged to raise money for any number of reasons: to exploit mineral resources or install electric light in the family mansion, to provide marriage portions for the daughter, or to buy a military commission for a younger son. A mortgage may indicate family enterprise, extravagance — or penury.

From the mid sixteenth century onwards surveys and rentals were compiled, listing estate tenants and their holdings, common rights, feudal duties, terms of tenancy, etc. Later landowners demanded accurate graphic representations of their lands and marches. Estate maps and accompanying schedules may show the names of owners and occupiers of properties. By the eighteenth century many estates were being accurately surveyed at a scale large enough (1:500 or larger) to show the shape of individual buildings and the smallest features of the landscape.

Leases specify the conditions of tenure of those who worked the land. The lease might be granted for a term of years or for lives (typically for three lives). The individual lives were identified with names, occupations and ages. But the lease would expire unexpectedly if famine or pestilence wiped out the three generations of the one family. Registers and copies of leases are to be found in the landowner's muniments; the tenant's copy seldom survives.

Used in conjunction with the census, probate records, etc, estate muniments enable the searcher to recreate an ancestor's world. The furlongs he ploughed in the open fields may still be identifiable as ridges and furrows on modern pastures; the hedges he planted may not yet have been replaced by barbed wire; and the ditches he dug may still drain and divide up the land. The site of every ancestor's home should be visited. The village may have vanished, the victim of deliberate depopulation or natural decay, but a ghost of the toft and croft he occupied may remain among the hollow-ways and cropmarks in the modern fields. But the substantial houses built by some more prosperous manorial tenants during the sixteenth and seventeenth centuries do survive, albeit much altered, in many village streets.

The records of businesses — factory, mill, mine, public utility, bank, inn, bakery, smithy, corner shop — include wage books, pensions ledgers, rentals of workers' houses, correspondence, legal papers, contracts of employment with job descriptions. An ancestor's place of work should be visited. It is possible that the machine he minded is still at work in an old-fashioned factory. Larger firms often have museums portraying the history of the company.

12. Local government

Local authorities regulate and organise many aspects of daily life. And every citizen — as ratepayer, elector, merchant, tradesman, teacher, scavenger, pauper, debtor, criminal or councillor — participates in, or is affected by, the workings of a variety of official bodies — county and borough council, commission of supply, civil parish, sanitary authority, poor law union, school board, turnpike trust, pensions committee, parochial board or district council. Records are usually held locally, by the relevant departmental officials, by successor authorities, or may have been deposited in the county record office or public library.

Minute books record the deliberations of governing councils and committees. Generations of local councillors and paid officials — their names, actions and opinions — are recorded as well as individual members of the community.

The court books (of boroughs) contain suit rolls as well as lists of parties and final decisions in legal cases, which can be supplemented by reference to the unbound bundles of petitions, examinations, bills and correspondence preserved by the clerk.

> Patrick Cantley . . . chapman . . . in . . . Elgine . . .
> wes . . . at night challenged be George Gordon . . .
> and Hellen Ogilvie his spous for the stealling frae
> them of Tuo pair of pleads . . . and ane Chamber
> pott . . . and being searched and dankered . . .
> taken reid hand with the Fang . . . to be taken to
> the pillar in the fish mercat and ther his louge to be
> nailled to the Trone [1698]

Individuals, families and groups of inhabitants frequently petition the authorities:

> Isobell Gaull Daughter of the deceased James Gaull Sometime Wheelwright in Elgin, & now Spouse to Robert McAndrew late Glover in Elgin & one of the Out Chelsea pensioners, presently in ... the Island of Jersey ... humble application ... for ... a Small pittance ... towards Enabling me for Setting out for, & arriveing at the Said Island of Jersey [1756]

Local authorities own large tracts of land — perhaps granted in medieval royal charters, or purchased to accommodate shambles, sewage works, cemetery or housing development. In the course of such transactions over many years, local authorities have acquired large collections of title deeds referring to previous generations of owners and occupiers.

A variety of registers record different aspects of an individual's life: registers of applications and warrants for the erection or alteration of buildings (mainly from the nineteenth century onwards but earlier in larger cities) are accompanied by collections of detailed plans showing the external appearance, site and internal accommodation of the property, which the family historian should visit.

Registers of admissions to public schools began to be generally kept following the educational reform of the 1870s. These record, in standard form, pupil's name, age, parentage and date of admission, and sometimes previous schools or reasons for leaving: 'Dead', 'gone to Canada'. The school log book may supplement register entries with notes on the conduct or capacity of an individual pupil:

> J. [Ramsay] Macdonald has passed well, but should attend to History [1883]

In private or charity school archives, older registers may contain unexpectedly candid comments on an ancestor's character: 'Dilligent but a dull scholar', 'Intractable', 'Stupid Bad Scholar', 'Trifling', 'Sly'.

The school archive (at the school or local record office) may also include governors' minutes, applications for free places, timetables, punishment registers, teachers' testimonials, fees registers and correspondence with parents.

Boys and girls were bound apprentice for a term of years to learn a trade — printer, shoemaker, smith, mechanic, etc. A formal agreememt (indenture) written out in duplicate — one copy each for the master and the child's parents — contained personal details of the master and the apprentice as well as the financial arrangements. The agreement may have been registered by borough or parish, particularly in the case of pauper children. Many of these unfortunates — a burden upon the poor rates — were disposed of as farm labourers and domestic servants or cynically apprenticed to master sweeps or owners of factories, mills and mines — cheap labour with no hope of acquiring a useful trade or skill. From 1710 to 1811 a government duty on apprenticeship indentures resulted in the compilation of registers (available at the Public Record Office).

Merchant guilds appeared in the eleventh century, enjoying a monopoly of trade within a borough; and prosecutions of unfree traders who attempted to set up in business did not finally come to an end until the nineteenth century. The medieval guilds fulfilled a variety of functions: chamber of commerce, trade association, friendly society, burial club, religious society, insurance company. In addition the guilds regulated prices and enforced trading standards. Craft guilds, formed to protect the interests of urban craftsmen, appeared during the thirteenth century. Guild records include minutes, lists of members and quest and search books, recording investigations into workmanship. Records should be sought at guild headquarters, Guildhall Library (for London guilds) or the local record office.

The origins of the trade union movement may be found in the burial clubs and friendly societies formed during the eighteenth and nineteenth centuries. Records are located at union headquarters or amongst the archives collected at Warwick University.

Conveyances of property, marriage contracts, commercial obligations and other legal documents were, from medieval times, submitted to the borough authorities for registration. In Scotland the notary public had a lucrative business drawing up legal instruments and recording copies in protocol books now preserved in the Scottish Record Office and local archives. From 1617, a particular register of sasines was inaugurated in the sheriffdoms with a general register in Edinburgh. Burgh registers were begun in 1681. The deeds recorded describe the feudal ceremony of sasine:

> Archibald Watson Bailzie ... went ... with me Notar publick ... and there Gave and Delivered heritable State Sasine reall Actuall & Corporall possession thereof to ... Charles Urquhart as Brother german and heir Served to the Deceast Duncan Urquhart by Deliverance ... of earth & Ston of the Ground of the Said Lands [1742]

Most sasines registers are held at the Scottish Record Office, but some burgh registers are deposited locally.

Registers of deeds were also maintained: for English boroughs; the lands of the Bedford Level from 1663; Middlesex from 1708; the ridings of Yorkshire from 1704 to 1735; and other local authorities.

Irish registration from 1708 was particularly comprehensive, recording not only lands and parties but also the terms of jointures, children's portions, marriage settlements, family descents, leases for specified lives, wills, etc.

Scottish administration was ahead of the remainder of Britain in maintaining registers of various legal transactions. To protect the interests of creditors by providing a record of the outcome of the legal process of diligence, local courts maintained particular registers of hornings and inhibitions, supplemented from 1602 by general (national) registers. A national register of tailzies (entails) was commenced in 1688. Claims of general and special service, establishing an individual's title as heir to a deceased person, can be found in Chancery records (in the Scottish Record Office) and burgh archives.

Local government is financed by rates levied on a valuation of properties within the town or parish. Valuation and assessment rolls describe houses and lands, naming owners and occupiers and indicating rates due. Compulsory rating in England and Wales dates from the poor law of 1601. An act of 1744 opened rate books to public inspection and many authorities began preserving documents from that date. Scottish burgh cess and stent rolls and county valuations provide lists of householders and tenants from the seventeenth century. The valuation of Irish property was undertaken by Sir Richard Griffith, commissioner of valuation from 1827 to 1868. The field, house and record of tenure books, in the Public Record Office, Dublin, preserve Griffith's idiosyncratic descriptions: of Alexander Wilson's 'neat little cottage well furnished' with its small garden rented by the year for £5 ('though worth seven guineas') in the townland of Corporation, Killybegs, County Donegal [1839].

The collection of rates is recorded in cash books, ledgers, floppy discs, etc. Some financial records exist from the fourteenth century. Cash books recording payments to the town chamberlain of mails and duties in Scottish burghs may exist from the sixteenth century.

Local officials — constable, overseer of the poor, surveyor of highways, market overlooker, inspector of nuisances, water bailiff, coal weigher, scavenger — kept accounts of income and expenditure.

Catherine McIntosh. D. & I. Decr 10 Paid Cab fare for Conveying the above named person from Cassieford to the Police Office ... 1s 6d [1913]

The constable was responsible for maintaining law and order in town and country. This ancient office, formerly under the supervision of the magistrates, was reformed in the 1830s and 1840s. Police authority archives, which may be stored at the police station, record the conduct of individual officers:

> Donald McCarter Constable of the 2^d District was found on the public Road in a State of beastly intoxication ... and was carried to the Police Station House ... Dismiss him from the office [1840]

and the officers themselves kept records:

> James Douglas. &. Donald Cameron Both Common Vagrents travling in the Countrey with littel Excus ... I took them, Into Custatey Last Night for feighting in ther Lodgings and Loked them up ... brought them Before Balies Wilson and Walker [1840]

An act of 1572 created the office in England and Wales of parochial overseer, who relieved the poor or found them suitable employment:

Vestry Dinner	10s 0d
20 Faggotts for Dame Wilshire	3s 9d
Paid Wm Hart for sitting up with Brownsell	2s 0d
Clothes for J. Andrews	9s 0d
	[1790]

The poor law was reformed in England and Wales in 1834. Unions of parishes erected workhouses to administer a system of indoor relief. In Scotland responsibility for the poor was transferred, in 1845, from kirk sessions to new parochial boards.

Information gleaned from registers of paupers, registers of visits to children and lunatics boarded out, registers of workhouse inmates and punishments, workhouse diet sheets and parochial board files, minutes and letter books may be combined to provide cradle-to-grave biographies of a searcher's less fortunate forebears. The inspector of the poor kept a journal of visits:

> Margt. Baxter Wisemans Lane 17th Nov [1847] ... found her very ill ... and as she has a young child ... agreed with Mrs Forsyth or Cumming to keep it at 2/6 a week

Jane Tomlinson alias Pollock or Johnston Frasers Lodgings 6 Dec 1848 her husband John Tomlinson alias Pollock was committed to jail for 14 days for rioting & she was *taken in labour* — ordered a midwife — she was delivered of a child — she belongs to Aberdeen her husband belongs to Birmingham goes about selling mats

Margaret Giels or Gatherer ... Ramsburn, Rothiemay Age 43 years ... 1870 This Pauper has ... been burdened with the support of her son Adam who has two of his fingers amputated in consequence of an injury by Machinery. Her son George is dead, and she gets no assistance from either of her other sons who are most notorious Poachers. Isabella has had 2 illegitimate children. All the daughters dress gaudily, but give little help to their Mother ... 1881 Re-admitted, and allowed 2/6 a week ... 1892 Been very Poorly. ordered dr. to get some Beef & Cordial ... 1893 allowance increased 6d per week ... 1896 Died

Many poor people, particularly the old and disabled, were relieved by almshouses and hospitals, whose registers record the lives — and deaths — of the inmates:

Mrs. Wright died this day at ¼ to 4 O'clock, of suffocation by a lump of beef ... During her stay in the Institution, she has been very peaceable, agreeable and inoffensive. She had a numerous circle of acquaintance by whom she was greatly respected [1837]

The clerk of a local authority often served as collector of national assessed taxes — on shops, windows, coats of arms, servants, horses, dogs and carriages. From 1904 vehicle registration files preserved detailed biographies of motor cars, lorries, tractors, buses, etc as well as the names of their owners, who are also recorded in registers of drivers' licences.

Correspondence files and letter books preserved by town, county and parish clerks are an undeservedly neglected source of family history. Local authority correspondence refers to individuals involved in an astonishing range of subjects: ARP, evacuation, farming, fishing, housing, military tribunals, murder, nursing, sport, silicosis, squatting, venereal disease.

13. Parliament

The records of Parliament are to be found at the House of Lords Record Office. Sessional papers reflect the range of Parliament's activities — law and order, industry, commerce, the environment, local government, education, the poor, etc — and large numbers of individuals are mentioned, for instance in evidence presented to committees:

> Mr. HERMAN JOHN FALK, called in ... ARE you the owner or partner in salt works at Meadow-bank in Winsford? — I am neither; I have been secretary to my father for 10 years ... He is the sole owner ... He is a German by birth ... In the year 1868 there was a great strike ... The employers ... combined against the strikers very strongly, but ... gradually gave way ... My father was determined to hold out ... and imported a large number of Germans ... They are most obedient and docile ... they are much more easily managed [1888]

The titles of private acts of Parliament are printed in the published series of statutes at large. The text of these acts may be accompanied by affidavits, reports, petitions and other evidential material. Private acts refer to estate settlement:

> vesting all the Lands and Hereditaments in the County of *Tipperary* ... late the Estate of *Godfrey Boate,* Esq; ... in Trustees, to be sold for Payment of the Debts of the said *Godfrey* [1729]

charitable trusts:

> establishing of the Lands given by *John Bedford's* Will to the perpetual Repair of Highways at Ailesbury [1597]

naturalisation:

> *Jacob Valk* son of Nicholas Valk by Ann his wife born at Westsanen in North Holland ... having ... given Testimony of his loyalty ... is hereby from henceforth Naturalized [1753]

divorce:

> to dissolve the Marriage of *Daniel Mathew* Esquire, with *Penelope Smith* his now Wife, and to enable him to marry again [1745]

Almost all petitions to the House of Commons, for the redress of grievances or for changes in public policy, have been destroyed — accidentally in the fire of 1834, and deliberately by systematic weeding until 1950. Petitions to the House of Lords have survived.

Ordinary men throughout England subscribed with their signatures and marks the protestation returns of 1642, vowing to 'maintaine & defend ... ye true Reformed Protestant Religion expressed in the doctrine of the Church of England ... the power and Priviledges of Parliament. The Lawfull Rights & Liberties of ye subiect ...' Some returns are held in the British Library or written into parish registers.

Official records of Scottish parliaments at the Scottish Record Office commence in 1466, but miscellaneous acts, instruments, ordinances, charters, etc survive from the twelfth century onwards. The family historian dare not ignore this important source, much of which is easy of access in the indexed volumes, 1124 to 1707, published by the record commissioners.

14. The public records

The growth of central government bureaucracy has advantages for the genealogist, whose ancestors may have served the state and whose official career records may be a prime source of biographical information, and the recruitment of troops and the administration of the armed forces have resulted in the creation of a large body of information for family historians. Records of central government may be searched at the Public Record Office in central London and at Kew. Confidentiality is protected by the thirty-year rule though access to some more sensitive records may be restricted for a longer period.

Records of men serving in the navy commence about 1660. Admiralty, Paymaster General's and Navy Board records include musters of ships' companies, description books, pay books, medal rolls, returns of officers' and seamen's services, ships' logs, correspondence files, medical department registers, etc. The documents detail a man's origins, age, physical description, service, battles, wounds and next of kin. Information about pensions to seamen and their families and to coastguards, civilian officials, artificers and labourers may be found in the records of Greenwich Hospital, the charitable institution for the navy. The main series of records date from the eighteenth century.

Records of the marines amongst War Office and Admiralty papers include description books, from about 1750, arranged by companies, showing name, age, birthplace and physical description; attestation forms, from 1790, arranged by date of discharge; lists of officers from 1760; correspondence files; minutes; and registers.

Records of men serving in the army commence about 1660, though various earlier references may be found among exchequer records and state papers. War Office and Paymaster General's records include muster books, pay lists, monthly returns, description books, medal rolls, pension books and discharge papers, referring to a soldier's service from attestation to discharge or death. Men of the fencibles, militia and volunteers are documented in both public and local records. Surveys of full- and half-pay officers, conducted in 1828-9 and 1847, returned particularly full biographical details, but the identification of an ancestor's regiment should be made from other sources, particularly family papers or legends, or from ephemeral items such as badges, campaign medals or battlefield souvenirs.

Soldiers' documents commencing about 1760 are arranged by regiments until 1873, then alphabetically by surnames:

> *Gibraltar 28th November 1856*
> REGIMENTAL BOARD ... for the purpose of
> verifying ... the Services, Conduct, Character ...
> of ... No *3367 Private Hugh Gillen* ...
> Age *24 7/12*
> Height *5* Feet *4* Inches
> Hair *Light Brown* ...
> Trade *Labourer* ...
> Intended Place of Residence *Glasgow*
> *Deserted 2d June ... 1855 ... Sentenced 84 days*
> *Imprisonment ...*
> *Not in possession of good Conduct Badge*
> MEDICAL REPORT. — ... *suffers from second-*
> *ary Syphilitic Symptoms which render him unable*
> *to perform his duty*

The histories of individual civil servants may be traced in the records they created in the course of their duties and in personnel files. The earliest bureaucrats are seldom named, but from the thirteenth century Chancery clerks wrote their surnames in the corners of the documents they had copied. The family papers of public servants may include documents relating to official duties or correspondence and diaries referring to the problems of the office — Pepys in his diaries and Hoccleve in his poetry preserve graphic accounts of the work and internal politics of their offices.

Official records of civil servants refer to salary as well as to exceptional payments: to Charles Trice Martin, a clerk (later an assistant keeper) at the Public Record Office,

> for that portion of the work ... materials for the
> History of Great Britain & Ireland ... which has
> been finished — £150 [1893]

absences and leave, or general conduct:

> Mr Martin has always discharged his duties with
> diligence and fidelity to the entire satisfaction of
> myself and of my predecessors — The retirement
> of so highly qualified an Officer will in fact be a
> distinct loss to the Department in which he has
> served so many years [1906]

During the middle ages the Chancellor filled the role of
secretary to the king. He heard petitions personally and his
Court of Chancery functioned as a civil service. Chancery issued
letters patent concerning grants of land, licences or pardons for
the alienation of property, presentations to benefices, denization
and the creation of peers; and letters close referring to pardons,
subsidies, family settlement, etc. From the fourteenth century
onwards Chancery clerks accepted private title deeds for
enrolment, copying the documents on to the dorse of the close
rolls. Enrolments include deeds of bargain and sale, trust deeds
and conveyances of charity estates, bankrupts' estates, annuities,
papist property, wills, arbitration awards, change of name,
naturalisation, and boundary settlements.

From 1876 solicitors could deposit unclaimed money in
Chancery when unable to discover the whereabouts of legatees
or next of kin — and these dormant funds have been the source
of many a family legend.

The Privy Council advised the monarch on administrative
matters, creating an archive of petitions, minutes, correspondence, inquisitions, etc (from the 1380s onwards and especially
for the sixteenth and seventeenth centuries) referring to recusants, justices of the peace, merchants, burgesses, clergymen,
schoolmasters — people at every level of society.

The office of the king's secretary became pre-eminent during
the reign of Henry VIII. The secretary advised the monarch on
domestic and foreign policy, and the records of the secretarial
office (known as state papers) refer to education, county
administration, agriculture, industry, the law, poor relief,
highways, recusancy, mustering of armed forces, heraldry,
genealogy, etc.

From 1782 the Secretary of State for the Home Department
became responsible for domestic policy. The secretary liaised
with magistrates, government spies and politicians concerning
law and order, factory conditions, aliens, trades unions, strikes,
riots, the penal system, child labour, etc, and very many
individuals are mentioned in the records.

The Board of Trade implemented measures affecting Britain's
merchant fleet. Merchant seamen may be named from 1747
onwards in ships' muster rolls and recorded agreements.
Certificates of competence of merchant navy officers began to be

registered during the nineteenth century: masters and mates in 1845; engineers in 1862; and skippers and mates of fishing boats in 1883. The main series of registers for ordinary seamen, begun under an act of 1835, give physical descriptions and personal information as well as names of ships and details of previous service. However, the Public Record Office holds only a ten per cent sample of post-1861 crew lists. The remainder of the collection was saved from the official weeders, but at the cost of dispersing the records — to the National Maritime Museum, selected local record offices, and the Memorial University of Newfoundland. Also among Board of Trade records are passenger lists — of individuals leaving Britain from 1890 onwards (the earlier lists were weeded) — and records of immigrants from 1878 onwards. Petitions from seamen and their dependants from 1780 to 1854 for assistance from Trinity House (the incorporation having official regulation of shipping) may be searched at the Society of Genealogists, London.

Between 1643 and 1660 Parliament closely investigated the estates of delinquents — king, church, nobles and gentlemen. Records of parliamentary surveys of Royalists' estates (naming tenants), fines imposed and confiscations of lands may be found at the Public Record Office, in local and specialist archives and among estate muniments.

Taxation records contain useful lists of names, and even the humblest members of a community may be included — albeit noted as 'not liable' on grounds of poverty. But all taxes are unpopular among those required to pay them (the collection of a poll tax in 1377-81 helped to spark off the Peasants' Revolt), and many men and women could, and did, avoid assessment and their names may not appear in the Exchequer lists. Subsidy rolls record money raised by taxing movable property. Lists of taxpayers are especially complete for the years 1295-1332 and 1524-5:

> Will[elmus] Sturdi h[abe]t duas oves [et] vale[n]t
> .xvi.d' [et] duas pelles [et] vale[n]t.viii.d'.
> S[umm]a .iii. ob[oli]. [et] q[u]a[drans]
> (William Sturdy ... 1¾d)
> Alic[i]a fil[ia] Ric[ardi] h[abe]t vna[m] vacca[m].
> [et] valet .iii.s'. [et] dimid[iam] sum[mam] auene.
> [et] valet. vi.d' S[umm]a. xva .iid'. [et] .iii.
> q[u]a[drantes]
> (Alice Richards ... 2¾d) [1225]

Exchequer fine rolls contain details of payments by individuals to the crown for privileges granted — wardship, letters of denization, pardons for trespass, and public office.

The Court of Wards and Liveries (1540-1660) exploited the

crown's feudal rights over tenants in chief and by knight service — their succession, wardship and marriage — as well as caring for the property of idiots and lunatics. Inquisitions *post mortem,* proofs of age and estate extents from the thirteenth century until 1660 provide details of tenants, heirs and property.

Tontines and annuity schemes were an effective and popular means of raising money. Eleven schemes were floated from 1693 to 1789, including the Irish tontines of 1773-7. Some thirty thousand subscribers and nominees are named in connection with the various schemes. The records include details of the marriages, deaths and wills of participants.

Customs records include collectors' particular accounts, from the late thirteenth century, and port books, from 1565, recording the names of ships, masters and merchants, as well as cargoes and destinations (port books for London for the years 1696-1795 were destroyed by official weeding). Correspondence of the Board of Customs survives from 1814 onwards. The letters refer to individual customs officials, for example:

> The Conduct of Henry Comper, a Boatman in absenting himself without leave ... from Drunkenness [1813]

Appointments are recorded — and promotions:

> James Sammes ... a Competent Tidewaiter ... in consequence of the insanity of Mr. Richard Chiverton Coastwaiter at Ryde [1813]

The family historian may expect to find records of ancestors attending the various law courts, as petitioners, witnesses, plaintiffs — if not as criminals. And, though a reference may provide no new limb to the pedigree, it will add flesh to the bones of an individual's biography.

Common law courts include King's Bench, Common Pleas, Exchequer — as well as circuit courts of assize, eyre, gaol delivery, oyer and terminer, and trailbaston. Equity courts include Chancery, Exchequer, Requests and Star Chamber. The records of the highest court in the land, Parliament, to which appeals from lower courts might be directed, are relatively complete from 1621 at the House of Lords Record Office.

Collections of deeds, wills, valuations, family settlements, dispositions, pedigrees and other documents may have been preserved as evidence in civil causes. Indictment files contain statements by witnesses, recognisances to appear in court, calendars of prisoners, inquisitions by coroners and grand jury presentments. Unfortunately, the files for the years since 1800 have been weeded. Calendars of prisoners for trial or under sentence were often printed for sale or published in the newspapers. Prisoners were also listed in the Newgate Calendar,

1782-1853, the records of the Fleet, Marshalsea and King's Bench prisons, 1685-1862, and miscellaneous criminal registers, 1791-1892. The Old Bailey functioned as an assize court for London from 1834, but sessions papers recording its work as the central criminal court are preserved from 1801.

Records of proceedings of the Court of Bankruptcy, which was founded in 1710, bankruptcy records of Chancery Petty Bag Office (including original records of certain firms for the period 1774-1830) and Exchequer extents and inquisitions referring to crown debtors, 1625-1842, can be supplemented with published lists of bankrupts from 1772. The dissolving of partnerships and commissions of bankruptcy are reported in the *London Gazette*. From 1824 records relating to insolvent debtors are also deposited with the clerk of the peace.

The High Court of Admiralty was concerned with cases of piracy and spoil from the fourteenth century onwards. The court assumed wide powers over shipping and merchandise around the coasts, considering cases of murder, assault, collision, wages, commercial disputes, insurance and salvage. Subsidiary local vice-admiralty courts heard similar cases. Records survive in national and local record offices.

The archive of the Court of Great Sessions for Wales, 1536-1830, is held at the National Library of Wales.

The Irish court records which survived the fire of 1922 are to be found in the Public Record Office of Ireland.

The records of Scottish departments of state may be searched at the Scottish Record Office. Departmental records before 1707 include Chancery, from about 1315; Privy Seal, from 1488; Privy Council, from 1545; Exchequer, from 1263; Crown Office writs, from 1147; and state papers, from 1326.

Following the Act of Union various boards and departments were established: manufactures, fishery, supervision for relief of the poor, education, post office. A main role of the Scottish Board of Excise was the prosecution of illegal distillers of *uisgebeatha* (whisky) — the water of life. The gaugers searched out illicit stills even in remote glens, though the distillers seem to have accepted frequent prosecution and fines almost with equanimity, as an inevitable penalty — a kind of taxation:

> William Leslie, Neither. ley, Rothes, Moray ...
> Discovered By T. Stephen ... Distilling privately
> & seized at Work one still, Penalty £500 ... Fines
> awarded 10s 6d [1816]

The principal Scottish court, the Court of Session, was endowed in 1532. Causes were also heard locally by circuit judges (justiciars). Records of justice eyres begin in 1493.

For the genealogist sheriff court records are a prime source.

The sheriff heard cases concerning probate, poinding, damages, contract, debt; the prosecution of political and religious dissidents; the clearances (where entire villages were summoned and evicted):

> John Fraser in tullock Gribbanbegg ... Patrick Cumming there ... John Cumming there ... James Cumming subtenant to the said John Cumming ... John Grant alias Glass ... Donald Stewart, miller in Avimore ... Jas. Mckdonald [alias] Buie there ... to flit & remove themselves Wives Bairns familys, servants Cottars Grasmen goods and gear furth and from their ... posessions [1766]

and a range of criminal offences:

> James MackKenzie theiff ... Did ... being lodged in John Mackie his barn where his servants were lying when they were all asleep aryse under Cloud and Silence of Night and brack open ane Chist Belonging to Donald Clunes servitor ... to be ... taken to the harbour ... And there to be imbarqued on boord of the first ship going for London And from thence to be transported to Barbadoes...

15. Further reading

This list contains some of the more useful books for the family historian. These describe genealogical methods as well as the types of records available and useful in compiling a family tree.

Detailed guides to archival collections, available from local record offices and specialist and national repositories, are not included in the bibliography.

The standard works of social and political history, for instance the *Oxford History of England* and the *Edinburgh History of Scotland,* are essential reading. Social histories such as T. C. Smout *A History of the Scottish People 1560 - 1830* (Collins, 1969), P. Laslett *The World We Have Lost* (Methuen, 1965), and E. P. Thomson *The Making of the English Working Class* (Gollancz, 1963) are invaluable sources for the periods covered. For the younger genealogist, series such as *One Day in ...* (Tyndall), *Past-into-Present* (Batsford), *History of the Modern World* (Macdonald Educational) and *Growing up in ...* (Batsford) are recommended as entertaining and informative background reading.

Contemporary novels and other literary works, political tracts, social surveys, etc, must not be neglected. For instance, the novels of Charles Dickens, Benjamin Disraeli, Elizabeth Gaskell and Charles Kingsley and *The Condition of the Working Class in England* by Friedrich Engels, first published in German at Leipzig in 1845, provide revealing glimpses into the social environment of early Victorian England. Illustrative of attitudes in the past are such works as Thomas Paine *The Rights of Man,* a seminal work first published in 1791-2, and Mary Wollstonecraft *A Vindication of the Rights of Woman,* 1792. Popular culture — the music-hall song and the broadside ballad — must not be ignored. Published editions of contemporary diaries, such as those of Francis Kilvert and James Woodforde, describe the lives of ordinary people in town and country.

For researching the upper classes the tedious erudition of Burke's *Landed Gentry* or Debrett's *Peerage* might be relieved by sampling the novels of Anthony Trollope. Genealogical periodicals include the *Genealogists' Magazine* and *Family History News and Digest.* Your family history society may publish a journal.

In the following lists books more appropriate to young people are marked*. Place of publication is London, unless given otherwise.

Archives

Camp, A. J. *Wills and Their Whereabouts.* Camp, fourth edition 1974.

Cornwall, J. *How to Read Old Title Deeds XVI-XIX Centuries.* Birmingham University Department of Extra-Mural Studies, Birmingham, 1964.

Cox, J., and Padfield, T. *Tracing Your Ancestors in the Public Record Office.* Her Majesty's Stationery Office, 1981.

Emmison, F. G. *Archives and Local History.* Methuen, 1966.

*Emmison, F. G. *Introduction to Archives.* British Broadcasting Corporation, 1964.

Emmison, F. G., and Gray, I. *County Records.* Historical Association, revised edition 1973.

Foster, J., and Sheppard, J. *British Archives: A Guide to Archive Resources in the United Kingdom.* Macmillan, 1982.

Galbraith, V. H. *An Introduction to the Use of Public Records.* Oxford University Press, Oxford, 1934.

Gibson, J. S. W.*Census Returns, 1841, 1851, 1861, 1871 on Microfilm: A Directory to Local Holdings.* Gulliver Press, Federation of Family History Societies, Banbury 1979.

Gibson, J. S. W. *Quarter Sessions Records for Family Historians: A Select List.* Federation of Family History Societies, Plymouth, 1982.

Gibson, J. S. W. *A Simplified Guide to Probate Jurisdictions.* Federation of Family History Societies, Plymouth, second edition 1981.

Gibson, J. S. W. *Wills and Where to Find Them.* Phillimore, for British Record Society, Chichester and London, 1981.

Gibson, J. S. W., and Peskett, P. *Record Offices: How to Find Them.* Federation of Family History Societies, Plymouth, 1981.

Hotten, J. *The Original Lists of Persons of Quality . . . Who Went from Great Britain to the American Plantations 1600-1700.* Chatto and Windus, 1874.

Iredale, D. *Enjoying Archives.* Phillimore, Chichester, second edition 1985.

MacFarlane, A. *A Guide to English Historical Records*. Cambridge University Press, Cambridge, 1983.

Martin, C. T. *The Record Interpreter*. Phillimore, Chichester, third edition 1982.

Owen, D. M. *The Records of the Established Church in England Excluding Parochial Records*. British Records Association, 1970.

Phillimore, W. P. W., and Fry, E. A. *An Index to Changes of Name 1760-1901*. Phillimore, 1905.

Redstone, L. J., and Steer, F.W. *Local Records: Their Nature and Care*. Bell, 1953.

Steel, D. J. *National Index of Parish Registers*. Phillimore, for Society of Genealogists, 1966-

Stephens, W. B. *Sources for English Local History*. Manchester University Press, Manchester, 1973.

Tate, W. E. *The Parish Chest*. Cambridge University Press, Cambridge, 1969.

West, J. *Town Records*. Phillimore, Chichester, 1983.

West, J. *Village Records*. Macmillan, 1962.

White, H. L. *Monuments and Their Inscriptions: A Practical Guide*. Society of Genealogists, 1977.

Whitmore, J. B. *A Genealogical Guide: An Index to British Pedigrees in Continuation of Marshall's Genealogist's Guide*. Society of Genealogists, 1953.

Whyte, D. *Introducing Scottish Genealogical Research*. Scottish Genealogy Society, Edinburgh, fifth edition 1984.

*Willis, A. J., and Tatchell, M. *Genealogy for Beginners*. Phillimore, Chichester, fifth edition 1984.

Chronology

Cheney, C. R. *Handbook of Dates for Students of English History*. Royal Historical Society, 1961.

Powicke, F. M. *Handbook of British Chronology*. Royal Historical Society, 1961.

Family history etc.

Barrow, G. B. *The Genealogist's Guide: An Index to Printed British Pedigrees and Family Histories 1950-1975*. Research Publishing Company, 1977.

Begley, D. F. *Irish Genealogy: A Record Finder*. Heraldic Artists, Dublin, 1981.

*Black, J. A. *Your Irish Ancestors: An Illustrated History of Irish Families and Their Origins*. Paddington Press, 1974.

Blythe, R. *Akenfield; Portrait of an English Village*. Allen Lane The Penguin Press, 1969.

Buckley, K. A. *Ancestry Tracing*. K. A. Buckley, Birmingham, 1978.

Burns, N. *Family Tree*. Faber, 1962.

Camp, A. J. *Everyone Has Roots: An Introduction to Genealogy*. W. H. Allen, Star Book, 1978.

Camp, A. J. *Tracing Your Ancestors*. John Gifford, 1970.

Clare, W. *A Simple Guide to Irish Genealogy*. Irish Genealogical Research Society, third edition by R. Ffolliott, 1966.

*Colwell, S. *The Family History Book*. Phaidon Press, Oxford, 1980.

*Colwell, S. *Tracing Your Family Tree*. Faber, 1984.

*Crush, M. *Trace Your Family Tree*. Granada, 1983.

Currer-Briggs, N. *Worldwide Family History*. Routledge and Kegan Paul, 1982.

*Currer-Briggs, N., and Gambier, R. *Debrett's Family Historian: A Guide to Tracing Your Ancestry*. Debrett's Peerage Limited and Webb and Bower, 1981.

Currer-Briggs, N., and Gambier, R. *In Search of Huguenot Ancestry*. Phillimore, Chichester, 1985.

Dixon, J. T., and Flack, D. D. *Preserving Your Past: A Painless Guide to Writing Your Autobiography and Family History*. Doubleday, New York, 1977.

Doane, G. H. *Searching for Your Ancestors: The How and Why of Genealogy*. University of Minnesota Press, Minneapolis, fourth edition 1973.

Evans, G. E. *From Mouths of Men*. Faber, 1976.

Ferguson, J. P. S. *Scottish Family Histories Held in Scottish Libraries*. Scottish Central Library, Edinburgh, 1960.

Ffolliott, R. *see* Clare, W.

FURTHER READING

Field, D. M. *Step-by-Step Guide to Tracing Your Ancestors*. Hamlyn, 1982.

Gardner, D. E., and Smith, F. *Genealogical Research in England and Wales*. Bookcraft, Salt Lake City, 1956-64.

Greenwood, V. D. *The Researcher's Guide to American Genealogy*. Genealogical Publishing Company, Baltimore, 1973.

Hamilton-Edwards, G. *In Search of Ancestry*. Phillimore, Chichester, fourth edition 1983.

Hamilton-Edwards, G. *In Search of Army Ancestry*. Phillimore, Chichester, 1977.

Hamilton-Edwards, G. *In Search of Scottish Ancestry*. Phillimore, Chichester, 1972.

Hamilton-Edwards, G. *In Search of Welsh Ancestry*. Phillimore, Chichester, 1985.

Humphery-Smith, C. R. *A Genealogist's Bibliography*. Phillimore, Chichester, new edition 1984.

Humphery-Smith, C. R. *The Phillimore Atlas and Index of Parish Registers*. Phillimore, Chichester, 1984.

James, A. *Scottish Roots: A Step-by-Step Guide for Ancestor-Hunters in Scotland and Overseas*. Macdonald, Loanhead, 1981.

Jones, V. L., Eakle, A. H., and Christensen, M. H. *Family History for Fun and Profit*. Genealogical Institute, Salt Lake City, revised edition 1972. (First appeared as *Genealogical Research: A Jurisdictional Approach*.)

Kyvig, D. E., and Marty, M. A. *Your Family History: A Handbook for Research and Writing*. AHM Publishing Corporation, Arlington Heights (Illinois), 1978.

Lichtman, A. J. *Your Family History: How to Use Oral History, Personal Family Archives, and Public Documents to Discover Your Heritage*. Random House, New York, 1978.

*Mander, M. *How to Trace Your Ancestors*. Granada, 1977.

Marshall, G. W. *The Genealogist's Guide*. New imprint of fourth revised edition 1903; Heraldry Today, 1967.

Matthews, C. M. *Your Family History: and How to Discover It*. Lutterworth, Guildford, 1976.

Montgomery-Massingberd, H. *Burke's Family Index*. Burke's Peerage, 1976.

Montgomery-Massingberd, H. *Burke's Irish Family Records*. Burke's Peerage, 1976.

Moss, W. W. *Oral History Program Manual*. Praeger, New York, 1974.

*Palgrave-Moore, P. *How to Record Your Family Tree*. Elvery Dowers, Norwich, 1979.

*Pelling, G. *Beginning Your Family History*. Federation of Family History Societies, Plymouth, 1980.

Pine, L. G. *The Genealogist's Encyclopedia*. David and Charles, Newton Abbot, 1969.

Pine, L. G. *Trace Your Ancestors*. Evans, second edition revised 1954.

Public Record Office. *Genealogy: A Selection of Leaflets*. Public Record Office, 1978-82 (PRO leaflets, 1 births, marriages, deaths; 2 census; 4 probate; 5 change of name; 6 immigrants; 7 emigrants; 8 shipping and seamen; 9a military; 18 Admiralty; 25 private conveyances; 26 apprenticeships; 28 Royal Marines; 30 Royal Irish Constabulary; 34 death duties; 37 genealogy from the public records).

Rayment, J. L. *Notes on the Recording of Monumental Inscriptions*. Federation of Family History Societies, Plymouth, second edition 1981.

Rogers, C. D. *The Family Tree Detective*. Manchester University Press, Manchester, 1983.

Shumway, G. L., and Hartley, W. G. *An Oral History Primer*. Deseret Book Company, Salt Lake City, 1974.

Society of Genealogists Leaflets: Number 3 'Family Records and Their Layout'; Number 4 'Note Taking and Keeping for Genealogists'; Number 7 'The Relevance of Surnames in Genealogy'; Number 9 'Starting Genealogy'; Number 12 'Army Muster and Description Books'. Society of Genealogists, 1977-82.

*Steel, D. J. *Discovering Your Family History*. British Broadcasting Corporation, 1980.

Steel, D. J., and Taylor, L. *Family History in Schools*. Phillimore, Chichester, 1973.

*Steel, D. J., and Taylor, L. *The Steels*. Nelson, Walton-on-Thames, 1976.
Thompson, P. *The Voice of the Past; Oral History*. Oxford University Press, Oxford, 1978.
Thomson, T. R. *A Catalogue of British Family Histories*. Research Publishing Company of London for Society of Genealogists, third edition 1980.
*Totten, E. *My Family Tree Book (for Colouring in Too)*. Evans, 1980.
Unett, J. *Making a Pedigree*. Second edition, David and Charles, Newton Abbot, 1971.
Vansina, J. *Oral Tradition: A Study in Historical Methodology*. Routledge and Kegan Paul, 1965.
Wagner, A. R. *English Ancestry*. Oxford University Press, Oxford, 1961.
Wagner, A. R. *English Genealogy*. Oxford University Press, Oxford, second edition 1972.

Heraldry

Brooke-Little, J. P. *Heraldry*. Blackwell, Oxford, 1975.
Burke, J. B. *The General Armory of England, Scotland, Ireland and Wales*. Harrison, London, 1878.
Elvin, C. N. *Hand-book of Mottoes*. Heraldry Today, revised edition 1971.
Fairbairn, J. *Fairbairn's Book of Crests of the Families of Great Britain and Ireland*. T. C. and E. C. Jack, Edinburgh, new edition, revised by A. C. Fox-Davies, 1892.
Fearn, J. *Discovering Heraldry*. Shire Publications, Princes Risborough, 1980.
Fox-Davies, A. C. *Armorial Families: A Complete Peerage, Baronetage, and Knightage*. Hurst and Blackett, seventh edition, 1929.
Fox-Davies, A. C. *A Complete Guide to Heraldry*. T. C. and E. C. Jack, London and Edinburgh, revised edition, 1909.
Fox-Davies, A. C. *Heraldry Explained*. Reprint of second edition of 1925, David and Charles, Newton Abbot, 1971.
Innes of Learney, T. *Scots Heraldry*. Oliver and Boyd, Edinburgh, second edition, 1956.
*Mackinnon, C. *The Observer's Book of Heraldry*. Frederick Warne, 1966.
*Manning, R. *Heraldry*. A. and C. Black, 1966.
*Moncreiffe, I., and Pottinger, D. *Simple Heraldry Cheerfully Illustrated*. John Bartholomew, London and Bromley, second edition, 1978.
Neubecker, O. *A Guide to Heraldry*. McGraw-Hill and Cassell, Maidenhead and London, 1979.
Papworth, J. W. *An Alphabetical Dictionary of Coats of Arms Belonging to Families in Great Britain and Ireland Forming an Extensive Ordinary of British Armorials; Upon an Entirely New Plan, in which the Arms are Systematically Subdivided* . . . T. Richards, 1874.
Pine, L. G. *Teach Yourself Heraldry and Genealogy*. The English Universities Press, 1957.
*Ralphs, D. H. *A First Look at Heraldry*. Franklin Watts, 1973.
Rogers, H. C. B. *The Pageant of Heraldry*. Seeley Service, 1957.
Scott-Giles, C. W., and Brooke-Little, J. P. *Boutell's Heraldry*. Frederick Warne, revised edition 1963.

Languages

Gooder, E. A. *Latin for Local History*. Longman, second edition, 1978.
Kelham, R. A. *A Dictionary of the Norman or Old French Language*. Edward Brooke, 1779; republished Tabard Press, East Ardsley, 1978.
Latham, R. E. *Revised Medieval Latin Word List*. Oxford University Press for British Academy, 1965.

Names

Bardsley, C. W. *A Dictionary of English and Welsh Surnames with Special American Instances*. Reprint of 1901 edition; Genealogical Publishing Company, Baltimore, 1980.
Black, G. F. *The Surnames of Scotland: Their Origin, Meaning and History*. Reprint of 1946 edition; Public Library and Readex Microprint Corporation, New York, 1979.

*Cottle, B. *The Penguin Dictionary of Surnames*. Penguin, Harmondsworth, second edition, 1978.

Guppy, H. B. *Homes of Family Names in Great Britain*. Harrison, 1890.

*Hassall, W. O. *History through Surnames*. Pergamon, Oxford, 1967.

MacLysaght, E. *Irish Families*. Hodges Figgis, Dublin, 1957.

MacLysaght, E. *More Irish Families*. Irish Academic Press, Black Rock, new edition 1982.

*MacLysaght, E. *The Surnames of Ireland*. Irish Academic Press, Dublin, fifth edition 1980.

Matthews, C. M. *How Surnames Began*. Lutterworth, Guildford and London, 1967.

Pine, L. G. *The Story of Surnames*. Country Life, 1965.

Pine, L. G. *They Came with the Conqueror*. Evans, 1954.

Reaney, P. H. *A Dictionary of British Surnames*. Routledge and Kegan Paul, second revised edition 1976.

Reaney, P. H. *The Origin of English Surnames*. Routledge and Kegan Paul, 1967.

*Verstappen, P. *The Book of Surnames*. Pelham, 1980.

Palaeography

Dawson, G. E., and Kennedy-Skipton, L. *Elizabethan Handwriting 1500-1650 : A Guide to the Reading of Documents and Manuscripts*. Faber, 1968.

Denholm-Young, N. *Handwriting in England and Wales*. University of Wales Press, Cardiff, second edition 1964.

Emmison, F. G. *How to Read Local Archives 1550-1700*. Historical Association, 1967.

*Grieve, H. E. P. *Examples of English Handwriting 1150-1750*. Essex Education Committee, Chelmsford, 1954.

Hector, L. C. *The Handwriting of English Documents*. Edward Arnold, 1958.

*Jackson, D. *The Story of Writing*. Cassell, Studio Vista, 1981.

Jenkinson, H. *The Later Court Hands in England from the Fifteenth to the Seventeenth Century*. Cambridge University Press, Cambridge, 1927.

Johnson, C., and Jenkinson, H. *English Court Hand, AD 1066 to 1500*. Clarendon Press, Oxford, 1915.

Newton, K. C. *Medieval Local Records : A Reading Aid*. Historical Association, 1971.

Parkes, M. B. *English Cursive Book Hands 1250-1500*. Oxford University Press, Oxford, 1969.

Simpson, G. G. *Scottish Handwriting 1150-1650*. Bratton, Edinburgh, 1973.

Whalley, J. I. *English Handwriting 1540-1853*. Her Majesty's Stationery Office, 1969.

Peerage, Baronetage etc.

Burke, J. *A General and Heraldic Dictionary of the Peerage and Baronetage*. 1826.

Burke, J. and J. B. *A Genealogical and Heraldic Dictionary of the Peerages of England, Ireland and Scotland, Extinct, Dormant and in Abeyance*. Henry Colburn, second edition, 1840.

Burke, J. *A Genealogical and Heraldic History of the Commoners... Enjoying Territorial Possessions* (later editions entitled *The Landed Gentry*). Henry Colburn, 1833-8.

Burke, J. and J. B. *A Genealogical and Heraldic History of the Extinct and Dormant Baronetcies of England*. Scott, Webster and Geary, 1838.

Cokayne, G. E. *Complete Baronetage*. W. Pollard and Company, Exeter, 1900-6.

Cokayne, G. E. *The Complete Peerage of England Scotland Ireland Great Britain and the United Kingdom, Extant Extinct or Dormant*. St Catherine's Press, 1910-59.

Debrett, J. *Debrett's Peerage of England, Scotland, and Ireland*. J. Debrett, 1803.

Paul, J. B. *The Scots Peerage*. David Douglas, Edinburgh, 1904-14.

16. Select list of record repositories and useful addresses

ABERDEEN University Library, Manuscripts and Archives Section, King's College, Aberdeen AB9 2UB.

City of Aberdeen District Archives, Town House, Aberdeen AB9 1AQ.

ANGUS District Council, Director of Administration, County Buildings, Forfar, Angus DD8 3LG.

ARGYLL AND BUTE District Archives, The Court House, Inveraray, Argyll PA32 8TX.

AVON Bath City Record Office, Guildhall, Bath BA1 5AW.

Bristol Record Office, Council House, College Green, Bristol BS1 5TR.

BEDFORDSHIRE Record Office, County Hall, Bedford MK42 9AP.

BERKSHIRE Record Office, Shire Hall, Shinfield Park, Reading RG2 9XD.

British Broadcasting Corporation, Written Archives Centre, Caversham Park, Reading RG4 8TZ.

Institute of Agricultural History and Museum of English Rural Life, University of Reading, Whiteknights, Reading RG6 2AG.

BIRMINGHAM Public Libraries, Archives Department, Chamberlain Square, Birmingham B3 3HQ.

Birmingham University Library, Special Collections Department, Main Library, PO Box 363, Birmingham B15 2TT.

BOLTON Metropolitan Borough Archives, Civic Centre, Le Mans Crescent, Bolton BL1 1SA.

BORDERS Regional Library, St Mary's Mill, Selkirk, TD7 5EU.

BRADFORD West Yorkshire Archive Service, Bradford District Archives, 15 Canal Road, Bradford BD1 4AT.

BUCKINGHAMSHIRE Record Office, County Hall, Aylesbury HP20 1UA.

Buckinghamshire Archaeological Society, County Museum, Church Street, Aylesbury HP20 2QP.

CALDERDALE West Yorkshire Archive Service (Calderdale), Central Library, Northgate House, Northgate, Halifax HX1 1UN.

CAMBRIDGESHIRE Record Office, Shire Hall, Castle Hill, Cambridge CB3 0AP, *and* Grammar School Walk, Huntingdon PE18 6LF.

Cambridge University Archives and University Library Department of Manuscripts, University Library, West Road, Cambridge CB3 9DR.

Churchill College Archives Centre, Churchill College, Cambridge CB3 0DS.

Peterborough Museum and Art Gallery, Priestgate, Peterborough PE1 1LF.

CENTRAL Regional Council Archives Department, Old High School, Spittal Street, Stirling FK8 1DG.

CHANNEL ISLANDS The Greffe, Royal Court House, St Peter Port, Guernsey.

La Société Guernesiaise, La Couture House, La Couture, St Peter Port, Guernsey.

The Judicial Greffe, Royal Square, St Helier, Jersey.

La Société Jersiaise Museum and Library, 9 Pier Road, St Helier, Jersey.

CHESHIRE Record Office, Duke Street, Chester CH1 1RL.

Chester City Record Office, Town Hall, Chester CH1 2HJ.

CLEVELAND County Archives Department, Exchange House, 6 Marton Road, Middlesbrough TS1 1DB.

CLWYD Record Office, Old Rectory, Hawarden, Deeside CH5 3NR, and 46 Clwyd Street, Ruthin LL15 1HP.

CORNWALL Record Office, County Hall, Truro TR1 3AY.

Royal Institution of Cornwall, County Museum, River Street, Truro TR1 2SJ.

COVENTRY City Record Office, Room 220, Second Floor, Broadgate House, Coventry CV1 1NG.

Warwick University Modern Records Centre, University Library, Coventry CV4 7AL.

CUMBRIA Record Office, The Castle, Carlisle CA3 8UR *and* County Offices, Kendal LA9 4RQ, and 140 Duke Street, Barrow in Furness LA14 1XW.

DERBYSHIRE Record Office, County Offices, Matlock DE4 3AG.

Derby Local Studies Library, Derby Central Library, Wardwick, Derby DE1 1HS.

RECORD REPOSITORIES

DEVON Record Office, Castle Street, Exeter EX4 3PQ.

Exeter Cathedral Library and Archives, Bishop's Palace, Exeter EX1 1HX.

Exeter University Library, Prince of Wales Road, Exeter EX4 4PT.

Federation of Family History Societies, 96 Beaumont Street, Milehouse, Plymouth PL2 3AQ.

West Devon Record Office, Unit 3, Clare Place, Coxside, Plymouth PL4 0JW.

DONCASTER Archives Department, King Edward Road, Balby, Doncaster DN4 0NA.

DORSET Record Office, County Hall, Dorchester DT1 1XJ.

DUDLEY Archives and Local History Department, Central Library, St James's Road, Dudley DY1 1HR.

DUMFRIES AND GALLOWAY Regional Council Library Service (Archives), Ewart Public Library, Catherine Street, Dumfries DG1 1JB.

DUNDEE District Archive and Record Centre, City Chambers, City Square, Dundee DD1 3BY (including Tayside Regional archives).

Dundee University Library, Archives Department, Dundee DD1 4HN.

DURHAM County Record Office, County Hall, Durham DH1 5UL.

Dean and Chapter Library, The College, Durham DH1 3EH.

Durham University, Department of Palaeography and Diplomatic, Prior's Kitchen, The College, Durham DH1 3EQ.

Local History Section, Darlington Branch Library, Crown Street, Darlington DL1 1ND.

DYFED Archive Service, Carmarthenshire Record Office, County Hall, Carmarthen SA31 1JP, and Ceredigion Area Record Office, Swyddfa'r Sir, Marine Terrace, Aberystwyth SY23 2DE, and Pembrokeshire Record Office, The Castle, Haverfordwest SA61 2EF.

National Library of Wales, Department of Manuscripts and Records, Aberystwyth SY23 3BU.

Royal Commission on Ancient and Historical Monuments in Wales and National Monuments Record, Edleston House, Queens Road, Aberystwyth SY23 2HP.

EAST SUSSEX Record Office, Pelham House, St Andrews Lane, Lewes BN7 1UN.

EDINBURGH District Archives, City Chambers, High Street, Edinburgh EH1 1YJ.

Edinburgh University Library, Special Collections Department, 30 George Square, Edinburgh EH8 9LJ.

General Register Office for Scotland, New Register House, Edinburgh EH1 3YT (births, marriages, deaths).

Lyon Office, New Register House, Edinburgh EH1 3YT.

National Library of Scotland, George IV Bridge, Edinburgh EH1 1EW.

National Museum of Antiquities, Country Life Archive, York Buildings, Queen Street, Edinburgh EH2 1JD.

Royal Commission on the Ancient and Historical Monuments of Scotland and National Monuments Record of Scotland, 54 Melville Street, Edinburgh EH3 7HF.

School of Scottish Studies, 27-28 George Square, Edinburgh EH8 9LD.

Scots Ancestry Research Society, 20 York Place, Edinburgh EH1 3EP.

Scottish Catholic Archives, Columba House, 16 Drummond Place, Edinburgh EH3 6PL (formerly Blair's College archives).

Scottish Genealogy Society, 21 Howard Place, Edinburgh EH3 5JY.

Scottish Record Office and National Register of Archives, PO Box 36, HM General Register House, Edinburgh EH1 3YY, and West Register House, Charlotte Square, Edinburgh EH2 4DF.

ESSEX Record Office, County Hall, Chelmsford CM1 1LX, *and* Southend Branch, Central Library, Victoria Avenue, Southend-on-Sea SS2 6EX.

FIFE St Andrews University, North Street, St Andrews KY16 9TR.

GATESHEAD Central Library, Prince Consort Road, Gateshead, Tyne and Wear NE8 4LN.

GLAMORGAN Archive Service, Glamorgan Record Office, Mid Glamorgan County Hall, Cathays Park, Cardiff CF1 3NE (for Mid, South and West Glamorgan).

National Museum of Wales, Welsh Folk Museum, St Fagans, Cardiff CF5 6XB.

Registrar General of Shipping and Seamen, Llantrisant Road, Llandaff, Cardiff CF5 2YS.

GLASGOW Business Archives Council of Scotland, Glasgow University Archives, The University, Glasgow G12 8QQ.

City of Glasgow, Mitchell Library, Rare Books and Manuscripts Department, 201 North Street, Glasgow G3 7DN.

Glasgow University Archives, The University, Glasgow G12 8QQ.

Glasgow University Library, Department of Special Collections, Hillhead Street, Glasgow G12 8QE.

See also Strathclyde.

GLOUCESTERSHIRE Record Office, Worcester Street, Gloucester GL1 3DW.

GRAMPIAN Regional Archives, Woodhill House, Ashgrove Road West, Aberdeen AB9 2LU.

GREATER MANCHESTER Record Office, 56 Marshall Street, New Cross, Ancoats, Manchester M4 5FU.

See also Manchester.

GWENT County Record Office, County Hall, Cwmbran NP4 2XH.

GWYNEDD Archives Service, Caernarfon Area Record Office, County Offices, Shirehall Street, Caernarfon LL55 1SH (archives located at Victoria Dock, Caernarfon LL55 1SR) *and* Dolgellau Area Record Office, Cae Penarlâg, Dolgellau LL40 2YB *and* Llangefni Area Record Office, Shire Hall, Llangefni LL77 7TW.

University College of North Wales Library, Department of Manuscripts, Bangor LL57 2DG.

HAMPSHIRE Record Office, 20 Southgate Street, Winchester SO23 9EF.

Portsmouth City Records Office, 3 Museum Road, Portsmouth PO1 2LE.

Southampton City Record Office, Civic Centre, Southampton SO9 4XL.

Southampton University Library, Southampton SO9 5NH.

HEREFORD AND WORCESTER Record Office, County Hall, Spetchley Road, Worcester WR5 2NP, *and* Hereford Record Office, The Old Barracks, Harold Street, Hereford HR1 2QX, *and* St Helen's Record Office, Fish Street, Worcester WR1 2HN.

HERTFORDSHIRE Record Office, County Hall, Hertford SG13 8DE.

HIGHLAND Regional Archive, Inverness Public Library, Farraline Park, Inverness IV1 1LS.

HUMBERSIDE County Record Office, County Hall, Beverley HU17 9BA.

Hull University, Brynmor Jones Library, Cottingham Road, Hull HU6 7RX.

South Humberside Area Record Office, Town Hall Square, Grimsby DN31 1HX.

Kingston upon Hull City Record Office, 79 Lowgate, Hull HU1 2AA.

IRELAND, REPUBLIC OF Public Record Office of Ireland, Four Courts, Dublin 7.

Chief Herald of Ireland, Genealogical Office, The Castle, Dublin.

Cork Archives Institute, Christchurch, Cork.

Dublin Corporation Archives, Dublin Public Libraries Archives Division, City Hall, Dame Street, Dublin 2.

Mid-West Regional Development Organisation, 104 Henry Street, Limerick.

National Library of Ireland, Kildare Street, Dublin 2.

Registrar General's Office, Custom House, Dublin.

Trinity College Library, College Green, Dublin 2.

University College Dublin, Archives Department, 82 St Stephen's Green, Dublin 2.

ISLE OF MAN Chief Registrar, General Registry, Finch Road, Douglas (births, marriages, deaths).

General Registry, Finch Road, Douglas (deeds, probate etc.).

Manx Museum Library, Kingswood Grove, Douglas.

ISLE OF WIGHT County Record Office, 26 Hillside, Newport, Isle of Wight PO30 2EB.

KENT Archives Office, County Hall, Maidstone ME14 1XQ, *and* South East Kent Branch, Folkestone Central Library, Grace Hill, Folkestone CT20 1HD, *and* Ramsgate Branch, Ramsgate Library, Guildford Lawn, Ramsgate CT11 9AY.

Canterbury Cathedral Archives and Library *and* City *and* Diocesan Record Office, The Precincts, Canterbury CT1 2EG.

Institute of Heraldic and Genealogical Studies, Northgate, Canterbury CT1 1BA.

KIRKLEES Church of Jesus Christ of Latter-Day Saints, Branch Genealogical Library, 12 Halifax Road, Huddersfield HD3 3BS.

West Yorkshire Archive Service (Kirklees), Central Library, Princess Alexandra Walk, Huddersfield HD2 2SU.

KNOWSLEY Library Information Services, Local Studies and Archives Collection, Knowsley Central Library, Derby Road, Huyton, Liverpool L36 9UJ.

LANCASHIRE Record Office, Bow Lane, Preston PR1 8ND.

Department of Health and Social Security, Archives Registry, Scholfield Mill, Brunswick Street, Nelson BB9 0HU.

LEEDS West Yorkshire Archive Service (Leeds), Chapeltown Road, Sheepscar, Leeds LS7 3AP.

Leeds University, Brotherton Library, Leeds LS2 9JT.

Yorkshire Archaeological Society, Claremont, Clarendon Road, Leeds LS2 9NZ.

LEICESTERSHIRE Record Office, 57 New Walk, Leicester LE1 7JB.

Leicester University Library, University Road, Leicester LE1 7RH.

LINCOLNSHIRE Archives Office, The Castle, Lincoln LN1 3AB.

LIVERPOOL Record Office, City Libraries, William Brown Street, Liverpool L3 8EW.

Liverpool University Archives, PO Box 147, Senate House, Abercromby Square, Liverpool L69 3BX.

Liverpool University, Sydney Jones Library, PO Box 123, Liverpool L69 3DA.

LONDON Army Records Centre, Bourne Avenue, Hayes, Middlesex UB3 1RF.

Barking and Dagenham Public Libraries, Valence Reference Library, Becontree Avenue, Dagenham, Essex RM8 3HT.

Barnet Public Libraries, Local History Library, Hendon Catholic Social Centre, Egerton Gardens, Hendon, London NW4 4BE.

British Architectural Library, Royal Institute of British Architects, Manuscripts Collection, 66 Portland Place, London W1N 4AD.

British Library, Department of Manuscripts, Great Russell Street, London WC1B 3DG.

British Library of Political and Economic Science, 10 Portugal Street, London WC2A 2HD.

British Museum (Natural History), Cromwell Road, London SW7 5BD.

British Records Association, Charterhouse, Charterhouse Square, London EC1M 6AU.

Bromley Public Libraries, Archives Section, Central Library, High Street, Bromley, Kent BR1 1EX.

Business Archives Council, Denmark House, 185 Tower Bridge Road, London SE1 2UF.

Camden Public Libraries, Swiss Cottage Library, 88 Avenue Road, London NW3 3HA, and Holborn Library, 32-38 Theobalds Road, London WC1X 8PA.

Catholic Central Library, 47 Francis Street, London SW1P 1DN.

Charity Commission for England and Wales, 14 Ryder Street, St James's, London SW1Y 6AH.

Church Commissioners, 1 Millbank, London SW1P 3JZ.

Church House Record Centre, Dean's Yard, London SW1P 3NZ (information on records of Church of England).

Church of Jesus Christ of Latter-Day Saints, Branch Library, Hyde Park Chapel, 64 Exhibition Road, London SW7 2PA.

City of London Polytechnic, Fawcett Library, Old Castle Street, London E1 7NT.

College of Arms, Queen Victoria Street, London EC4V 4BT.

Corporation of London Records Office, PO Box 270, Guildhall, London EC2P 2EJ.

Dr Williams's Library, 14 Gordon Square, London WC1H 0AG (nonconformist records).

Duchy of Cornwall Office, 10 Buckingham Gate, London SW1E 6LA.

Ealing Borough Libraries, Central Library, Walpole Park, Ealing, London W5 5EQ.

Greater London Record Office, 40 Northampton Road, London EC1R 0HB.

Greenwich Local History Library and Archives, Woodlands, 90 Mycenae Road, Blackheath, London SE3 7SE.

Guildhall Library, Aldermanbury, London EC2P 2EJ.
Guild of One-name Studies, 15 Cavendish Gardens, Cranbrook, Ilford IG1 3EA.
Hackney Library Services, Archives Department, Rose Lipman Library, De Beauvoir Road, London N1 5SQ.
Hammersmith and Fulham Public Libraries, Archives Department, Shepherd's Bush Library, 7 Uxbridge Road, London W12 8LJ.
Haringey Libraries, Museum and Arts Department, Bruce Castle Museum, Lordship Lane, London N17 8NU.
Her Majesty's Customs and Excise, Library Services, Room 428, King's Beam House, Mark Lane, London EC3R 7HE.
Honourable Society of Cymmrodorion, 118 Newgate Street, London EC1A 7AE (Welsh genealogy).
House of Lords Record Office, House of Lords, London SW1A 0PW.
Imperial College of Science and Technology Archives, Room 455, Sherfield Building, Imperial College, London SW7 2AZ.
Imperial War Museum, Department of Documents, Lambeth Road, London SE1 6HZ.
India Office Library and Records, Foreign and Commonwealth Office, 197 Blackfriars Road, London SE1 8NG.
Institute of Geological Sciences Library, Exhibition Road, London SW7 2DE.
Institution of Civil Engineers Library, Great George Street, Westminster, London SW1P 3AA.
Institution of Electrical Engineers, Archives Department, Savoy Place, London WC2R 0BL.
Islington Libraries Archives and Local History Collections, Finsbury Library, 245 St John Street, London EC1 4NB, *and* Islington Central Library, 2 Fieldway Crescent, London N5 1PF.
Kensington and Chelsea Public Libraries, Central Library, Phillimore Walk, London W8 7RX.
Lambeth Archives Department, Minet Library, 52 Knatchbull Road, London SE5 9QY.
Lambeth Palace Library, London SE1 7JU.
Lewisham Archives and Local History Department, The Manor House, Old Road, Lee, London SE13 5SY.
Linnean Society of London, Burlington House, Piccadilly, London W1V 0LQ.
Manorial Documents Register, Quality House, Quality Court, Chancery Lane, London WC2A 1HP.
Museum of London, London Wall, London EC2Y 5HN.
National Army Museum, Department of Records, Royal Hospital Road, London SW3 4HT.
National Maritime Museum, Manuscripts Section, Greenwich, London SE10 9NF.
National Register of Archives, Quality House, Quality Court, Chancery Lane, London WC2A 1HP.
Newham Local Studies Library, Stratford Reference Library, Water Lane, London E15 4NJ.
Office of Population Censuses and Surveys, General Register Office, St Catherine's House, 10 Kingsway, London WC2B 6JP (births, marriages) *and* Alexandra House, 31 Kingsway, London WC2B 6UF (deaths).
Post Office Archives, Freeling House, 23 Glass Hill Street, London SE1 0BQ.
Principal Registry of the Family Division, Somerset House, Strand, London WC2R 1LP (wills).
Public Record Office, Ruskin Avenue, Kew, Richmond, Surrey TW9 4DU *and* Chancery Lane, London WC2A 1LR.
Religious Society of Friends' Library, Friends House, Euston Road, London NW1 2BJ.
Royal Air Force Museum, Department of Archives and Aviation Records, Aerodrome Road, Hendon, London NW9 5LL.
Royal Army Medical College, Muniment Room, Millbank, London SW1 4RJ.
Royal Botanic Gardens, Library and Archives, Kew, Richmond, Surrey TW9 3AB.
Royal College of Physicians of London, 11 St Andrew's Place, Regent's Park, London NW1 4LE.

RECORD REPOSITORIES

Royal College of Surgeons of England, 35-43 Lincoln's Inn Fields, London WC2A 3PN.

Royal Commission on Historical Manuscripts, Quality House, Quality Court, Chancery Lane, London WC2A 1HP.

Royal Commission on Historical Monuments, England, *and* National Monuments Record, Fortress House, 23 Savile Row, London W1X 1AB.

Royal Institution of Great Britain, 21 Albemarle Street, London W1X 4BS.

Royal Society Library, 6 Carlton House Terrace, London SW1Y 5AG.

Science Museum Library, South Kensington, London SW7 5NH.

Society of Antiquaries of London, Burlington House, London W1V 0HS.

Society of Genealogists, 14/15 Charterhouse Buildings, London EC1M 7BA.

Southwark Local Studies Library, 211 Borough High Street, London SE1 1JA.

United Reformed Church History Society, 86 Tavistock Place, London WC1H 9RT.

University College London, Manuscripts Room, DMS Watson Library, Gower Street, London WC1E 6BT.

University of London Library, Senate House, Malet Street, London WC1E 7HU.

Victoria and Albert Museum Library, Cromwell Road, London SW7 2RL.

Waltham Forest Archives and Local History Collection, Vestry House Museum, Vestry Road, Walthamstow, London E17 9NH.

Wellcome Institute for the History of Medicine, 183 Euston Road, London NW1 2BP.

Westminster Abbey Muniment Room and Library, London SW1P 3PA.

Westminster City Libraries, Archives Department, Victoria Library, Buckingham Palace Road, London SW1W 9UD, *and* Local History Library, Marylebone Library, Marylebone Road, London NW1 5PS.

Westminster Diocesan Archives, Archbishop's House, Ambrosden Avenue, London SW1P 1QJ (Roman Catholic records).

MANCHESTER City Archives Department, Central Library, St Peter's Square, Manchester M2 5PD.

John Rylands University Library of Manchester, Deansgate, Manchester M3 3EH (includes Methodist archives).

North Western Museum of Science and Industry, 97 Grosvenor Street, Manchester M1 7HF.

See also Greater Manchester

MERSEYSIDE County Archives Service, 64-66 Islington, Liverpool L3 8LG.

MORAY District Record Office, Tolbooth, Forres, Moray IV36 0AB.

NITHSDALE District Council Archives, Municipal Chambers, Buccleuch Street, Dumfries DG1 2AD.

NORFOLK Record Office, Central Library, Norwich NR2 1NJ.

NORTHAMPTONSHIRE Record Office, Delapré Abbey, Northampton NN4 9AW.

British Steel Corporation, Records Services Section, East Midlands Regional Records Centre, By-Pass Road, Irthlingborough, Wellingborough NN9 5QH.

Northampton Central Library, Abington Street, Northampton NN1 2BA.

NORTHERN IRELAND Public Record Office of Northern Ireland, 66 Balmoral Avenue, Belfast BT9 6NY.

General Register Office, 49-55 Chichester Street, Belfast BT1 4HL (births, marriages, deaths).

NORTHUMBERLAND Record Office, Melton Park, North Gosforth, Newcastle upon Tyne NE3 5QX, *and* Berwick-upon-Tweed Record Office, Council Offices, Wallace Green, Berwick-upon-Tweed TD15 1ED.

NORTH YORKSHIRE County Record Office, County Hall, Northallerton DL7 8SG.

York City Archives Department, Art Gallery Building, Exhibition Square, York YO1 2EW.

York Minster Library, Dean's Yard, York YO1 2JD.

York University, Borthwick Institute of Historical Research, St Anthony's Hall, Peasholme Green, York YO1 2PW.

NOTTINGHAMSHIRE Record Office, County House, High Pavement, Nottingham NG1 1HR.

Nottingham University Manuscripts Department, University Library, University Park, Nottingham NG7 2RD.

ORKNEY The Orkney Library, Archives Department, Laing Street, Kirkwall KW15 1NW.

OXFORDSHIRE County Record Office, County Hall, New Road, Oxford OX1 1ND.

Bodleian Library, Department of Western Manuscripts, Oxford OX1 3BG.

Oxford University Archives, Bodleian Library, Oxford OX1 3BG.

PERTH AND KINROSS District Council Archive, Sandeman Library, 16 Kinnoull Street, Perth PH1 5ET.

Perth Museum and Art Gallery, George Street, Perth PH1 5LB.

POWYS County Council, County Libraries Headquarters, Cefnllys Road, Llandrindod Wells LD1 5LD.

RENFREW District Libraries Archives Service, Old Library, Collier Street, Johnstone, Renfrewshire PA5 8AR.

ROTHERHAM Metropolitan Borough, Brian O'Malley Central Library and Arts Centre, Walker Place, Rotherham, South Yorkshire S65 1JH.

SALFORD Archives Centre, 658/662 Liverpool Road, Irlam, Manchester M30 5AD.

SANDWELL Metropolitan Borough Council, Smethwick District Library, High Street, Smethwick, Warley, West Midlands B66 1AB.

SHEFFIELD City Libraries, Archive Division, Central Library, Surrey Street, Sheffield S1 1XZ.

Sheffield University Library, Western Bank, Sheffield S10 2TN.

SHETLAND Archives, 44 King Harold Street, Lerwick ZE1 0EQ.

SHROPSHIRE Record Office, Shire Hall, Abbey Foregate, Shrewsbury SY2 6ND.

SOMERSET Record Office, Obridge Road, Taunton TA2 7PU.

SOUTH TYNESIDE Central Library, Local History Department, Catherine Street, South Shields, Tyne and Wear NE33 2PE.

SOUTH YORKSHIRE County Record Office, Cultural Activities Centre, Ellin Street, Sheffield S1 4PL.

STAFFORDSHIRE Record Office, County Buildings, Eastgate Street, Stafford ST16 2LZ.

Burton-on-Trent Library, Riverside, High Street, Burton-on-Trent DE14 1AH.

Keele University Library, Keele ST5 5BG.

Lichfield Joint Record Office, Public Library, Bird Street, Lichfield WS13 6PN.

William Salt Library, Eastgate Street, Stafford ST16 2LZ.

STOCKPORT Library of Local Studies, Central Library, Wellington Road South, Stockport SK1 3RS.

STRATHCLYDE Regional Archives, Mitchell Library, North Street, Glasgow G3 7DN, *and* Ayrshire Subregion Archives Office, County Buildings, Ayr KA7 1DR.

See also Glasgow

SUFFOLK Record Office, Ipswich Branch, County Hall, Ipswich IP4 2JS, *and* Bury St Edmunds Branch, School Hall Street, Bury St Edmunds IP33 1RX *and* Lowestoft Branch, Central Library, Clapham Road, Lowestoft NR32 1DR.

SURREY Record Office, County Hall, Penrhyn Road, Kingston upon Thames KT1 2DN, *and* Guildford Muniment Room, Castle Arch, Guildford GU1 3SX.

TAMESIDE Local Studies Library, Stalybridge Library, Trinity Street, Stalybridge, Cheshire SK15 2BN.

TYNE AND WEAR Archives Department, Blandford House, West Blandford Street, Newcastle upon Tyne NE1 4JA, *and* Local Studies Centre, Howard Street, North Shields NE30 1LY.

UNITED STATES OF AMERICA Genealogical Department Library, Church of Jesus Christ of Latter-Day Saints, 50 East North Temple, Salt Lake City, Utah 84150.

WAKEFIELD District Library Headquarters, Balne Lane, Wakefield WF2 0DQ.

WALSALL Archives Service, Central Library, Lichfield Street, Walsall WS1 1TR.

WARWICKSHIRE Warwick County Record Office, Priory Park, Cape Road, Warwick CV34 4JS.

Shakespeare Birthplace Trust Records Office, Henley Street, Stratford-upon-Avon CV37 6QW.
WESTERN ISLES Island Council, Sandwick Road, Stornoway, Lewis PA87 2BW.
WEST SUSSEX Record Office, County Hall, West Street, Chichester PO19 1RN.
WEST YORKSHIRE Archive Service (Headquarters), Registry of Deeds, Newstead Road, Wakefield WF1 2DE.
See also Bradford, Calderdale, Kirklees, Leeds, Wakefield.
WIGAN Record Office, Town Hall, Leigh, Lancashire WN7 2DY.
WILTSHIRE Record Office, County Hall, Trowbridge BA14 8JG.
WIRRAL Archive Service, Reference and Information Services, Birkenhead Central Library, Borough Road, Birkenhead, Merseyside L41 2XB.
WOLVERHAMPTON Borough Archives, Central Library, Snow Hill, Wolverhampton WV1 3AX.

Index

* denotes two or more relevant references on the page.
See relevant subject heading for information on England, Ireland, Scotland and Wales.